Lectionary Worship Aids

Series VIII, Cycle A

Cradled In God's Heart

Thom M. Shuman

CSS Publishing Company, Inc., Lima, Ohio

LECTIONARY WORSHIP AIDS, SERIES VIII, CYCLE A

Copyright © 2007 by
CSS Publishing Company, Inc.
Lima, Ohio

Scripture quotations are from the New Revised Standard Version of the Bible, copyright
1989 by the Division of Christian Education of the National Council of the Churches of
Christ in the USA. Used by permission.

Library of Congress Cataloging-in-Publication Data

Shuman, Thom M.
    Lectionary worship aids : cradled in God's heart. Series VIII / Thom M. Shuman.
    p. cm.
    ISBN 0-7880-2456-6 (perfect bound : alk. paper)
 1. Worship programs. 2. Common lectionary (1992) I. Title.

BV198.R29 2007
264—dc22

2007007735

For more information about CSS Publishing Company resources, visit our website at
www.csspub.com or email us at csr@csspub.com or call (800) 241-4056.

Cover design by Barbara Spencer
ISBN-13: 978-0-7880-2456-6
ISBN-10: 0-7880-2456-6   PRINTED IN USA

For Bonnie,
and for Teddy:
gracious cradlers
of my life
and God's greatest gifts

*It ain't those parts
of the Bible
that I can't understand
that bother me;
it is the parts
that I do understand.*

— Mark Twain

Table Of Contents

Introduction

In the spring of 2001, through the generosity of the Lilly Endowment's Clergy Renewal Grant Program, I was able to spend three months away from the church I am blessed to serve. It truly was a time of renewal and refreshment for me, with a month spent at the Abbey of Gethsemane, a month at Iona, and time at the Taizé Community, Lindisfarne, and the Northumbria Community, as well.

In addition to the opportunities I had to worship without being the leader/preacher, I also had the time to spend in significant moments of reflection and silence, as well as being embraced by a variety of worship experiences and new forms of spirituality. One of the most significant experiences was that I began to tap into those words, those images, those people I met during those three months, and the deep well of grace God provides for each of us.

And so I began a season of writing. I began a weblog (www.occasionalsightings.blogspot.com) to share with others my spiritual journey and struggles. Being a lectionary preacher, I began to immerse myself in the weekly readings, not just for sermons, but for my spiritual growth as well. What began as tentative attempts to write pastoral prayers based on the readings, blossomed into a discipline of writing a new liturgy each week (as well as a poem/prayer for the back of the bulletin). This book is the compilation of those liturgies for the first year (A) in the lectionary cycle. I am grateful to CSS Publishing for providing the opportunity to share these liturgies with a wider audience.

A word about some of the "terms" I use in my liturgies. I have always been uncomfortable with the idea of "invoking" God's presence in worship, since God is already waiting for us, and so I write a Prayer Of The Day. I also believe that one of the marvelous things that happens in the act of confession is that we are reminded of how we are reconciled to God through the gift of Jesus Christ. And so, I think we should "call" people to this time of reconciliation. Some of the liturgies contain a Great Prayer Of Thanksgiving, as well. The church I serve does not celebrate communion each week, but I have put them in for special days in the life of the church.

I hope that you will find these words helpful in the worship life of your congregation.

— Thom M. Shuman

Advent 1

Isaiah 2:1-5
Romans 13:11-14
Matthew 24:36-44

Call To Worship

One: In the days to come, we will hear God calling us
**All: to lay aside our usual way of doing business;
to learn God's way of peace and hope.**
One: In the days to come, we will learn what time is,
**All: the time when God is coming,
not to destroy, but to restore;
not to take away, but to give.**
One: In the days to come, we will understand
**All: that God is coming to us,
not to empty our homes of their valuables, but to fill
our hearts with love;
not to judge, but to bless.**

Prayer Of The Day

Carver of Mountains and Architect of Cities,
as we begin our Advent journey,
may we learn what it is that you have to teach us,
that you who shapes time holds all our moments in your heart;
that you who knows our darkest past leads us into your bright future.

Jesus Christ,
you are the garment of grace,
which we put on
to protect us from the icy gales of death,
and sin's cruel grasp.

Spirit of Advent,
you draw us toward the approaching One,
reshaping our weapons into garden tools;

9

melting our frozen hearts into streams of love;
transforming our fears into faith.

God in Community, Holy in One,
may we see you coming toward us in these days,
even as we pray as Jesus taught us, saying,
   Our Father ...

Call To Reconciliation

This holiest of seasons may be the hardest time to be a believer. The clang of cash registers can silence the songs of angels; the promotions of the stores can lure us from the promise of new birth. Let us confess our need to become more and more like children in these days — hopeful, trusting, expectant.

Unison Prayer Of Confession

It is never easy to approach you with our confessions, God, our Advent. We know the way to the best bargains at the malls, but lose our way to you. We are quick to set down our calling whenever our desires get in the way. We are arrogant enough to believe that we are not the ones who have to worry when you come again.

Help us to lay aside all our pride, our faults, and our sins so our emptiness might be filled with your grace and hope, God of our days. Waken us to the bright dawn that is streaming over the horizon; alert us to the good we can do for others; ready us for the day that is coming when we will be reconciled to all people through the grace of our Lord and Savior, Jesus Christ.

Silence is kept

Assurance Of Pardon

One: A new season of Advent begins with the old promise; God has been with us, God is with us, God will remain with us; forgiving, healing, reconciling.

All: **We are loved, and called to love. We are forgiven, and gifted to forgive. We are transformed, and can transform the world. Thanks be to God. Amen.**

Advent 2

Isaiah 11:1-10
Romans 15:4-13
Matthew 3:1-12

Call To Worship

One: We gather, in this place, in this time of worship
All: to hear God's word that it might shape our voices.
One: We gather, with these people, in this season of preparation
**All: to see them as Jesus does,
              so we can live with one another.**
One: We gather, around this table in these Advent moments
**All: to drink of God's joy and peace,
              to be filled with the bread of hope.**

Prayer Of The Day

Glorious God,
you alone can stun us with your miracles;
children of grace born to those
with stone-cold souls;
antagonists serving one another
at the table of abundant joy;
discordant and angry voices becoming
a choir of harmony and peace.

Jesus Christ, Root of Jesse,
you plead the case of the poor
to a society
that has judged them;
you call us to play fair
with those whose gifts
we do not recognize;
you invite us to offer a square deal
to those who have been broken
by the bullies of the world.

11

Holy Spirit of hope,
may your wisdom rest upon us
so we might rely on God's word
and not our own;
may your guidance wrap around our shoulders,
so we might find the way to the kingdom;
may your awareness settle deep within us,
so that we may see those around us.

God in Community, Holy in One,
hear us as we pray as Jesus has taught us, saying,
Our Father ...

Call To Reconciliation

Powerful enough to judge us, the one coming toward us humbles himself in order to redeem us. He comes to baptize us with the living waters of hope, and to dry us off with the servant's towel wrapped around his waist. Let us confess our sins, repent, and welcome into our hearts the grace God offers to us in Jesus Christ.

Unison Prayer Of Confession

Steadfast God, how easy it is to lose our way in this season. Coddled in luxury's lap, we forget those who have no warmth, no food, and no home. At Christmas parties, we join in the ridicule of the needy, rather than setting free our friends (and ourselves) of prejudices. We drive around looking at the decorated houses, not noticing the people passing by who are searching for your kingdom.

We come to the living waters, Merciful God, to repent and be made whole. Baptize us anew with passion for the poor, with desire to serve your people, with willingness to follow the one who leads us into the future of your hope and peace, Jesus Christ, our Lord and Savior.

Silence is kept

Assurance Of Pardon

One:　The good news is that God listens to our hearts, and sees deep into our souls; God knows our desire to be faithful people, and fills us with the gifts to be God's children.

All:　**Like a soft rain on a summer's day, like a downpour in the midst of a drought, God's grace and mercy restore us, refresh us, make us anew. Thanks be to God! Amen.**

Advent 3

Isaiah 35:1-10
James 5:7-10
Matthew 11:2-11

Call To Worship
One: Be patient!
the time is coming
when we will celebrate the birth of Christ,
All: **when we will sing and rejoice,**
dancing with everlasting joy.
One: But for now,
let us wait in this season of Advent,
All: **when God speaks in dreams and visions,**
when we are invited to dance into the kingdom.
One: For this is Advent,
when all the world rejoices in its creator,
All: **when those who limp learn new dance steps,**
when the speechless burst forth with
joy to the world**!**

Prayer Of The Day
God,
using the unnoticed,
you accomplish the unexpected
for an uncaring world;
with the bread of life,
you restore the brokenness
of your creation;
letting go of your Child,
you fill our emptiness
with grace beyond measure.

Ever-new, always scarred, Jesus Christ,
in you, those silenced by the world

hear the whispers of angels
bringing good news;
in you, those shoved to the side
lead the race into the kingdom;
in you, those who grope in darkness
are firmly clasped by your love.

Advent's Spirit,
you fill the voiceless with the promises of your word;
you lead us out of exile,
placing God's beloved kin on the holy way to freedom,
not letting a single one of us lose our way.

God in Community, Holy in One,
hear us as we lift the prayer Jesus has taught us, saying,
   Our Father ...

Call To Reconciliation
   In this holiest of seasons, we can become so cynical: to doubt, to wonder, to question. In this time of bright lights and celebration, we can be blinded to the need around us. It is easy to grumble about what we do not have, rather than hearing the songs of children. Let us confess how we lose our way during this time, so that God will forgive us and put us back on the holy way.

Unison Prayer Of Confession
   God of hopes and joys, because it is easy for us to forget what you have done for us in the birth of Jesus, we can step off your path and wander the streets of the world. Our indifference keeps us from seeing those overlooked by our culture. Our fear keeps us from reaching out for your future. Our grumbling silences the angel speaking to us of your coming toward us.

   Forgive us, God of Advent. Fill our emptiness with the everlasting joy of your grace. Blow away our arrogant attitudes with your Spirit of compassion. Embolden our hearts with the courage of your Child, Jesus Christ, who became one of us so we might be your redeemed forever.

15

Silence is kept

Assurance Of Pardon

One: Be strong, do not fear! Our God is here! Your eyes will be opened to see God's salvation coming to you.

All: **Our spirits rejoice in God our Savior, who has called us blessed. Thanks be to God. Amen.**

Blessing

One: Go into the world,
          to see the kingdom which is in your midst,

All: **to hear the joy breaking forth in our lives;**
          to bear the good news to everyone we meet.

Advent 4

Isaiah 7:10-16
Romans 1:1-7
Matthew 1:18-25

Call To Worship
One: We gather in preparation
All: for good news is about to be proclaimed.
One: We gather in expectation
All: for joy is about to explode in our midst.
One: We gather in celebration
**All: for we are those people who have said
        yes to the manger,
        yes to love enfleshed,
        yes to the One incarnate for others,
        yes to the wholeness of God.**
One: With preparation and in expectation,
All: let us celebrate!

Prayer Of The Day
If our lives are dry and parched,
Lord God,
send the living waters of your Spirit
to revive us, to enliven us,
to bring forth new life.
Immanuel, come quickly.

If our times are empty and barren,
God of Creation,
grant us a rich harvest.
Send us home with sheaves of blessings,
fill us with your abundance,
and teach us to share the harvest with others.
Immanuel, come quickly.

If our bodies are weary and heavy laden,
Exuberant God,
fill us with laughter.
Give us shouts of joy,
envelop us with your gladness.
Immanuel, come quickly.

If our lives are small and trivial,
Majestic God,
make us see great things;
enlarge our vision,
widen our horizons.
Immanuel, come quickly,
even as we pray as you have taught us, saying,
Our Father ...

Call To Reconciliation

How can we prepare the way of the coming one into our hearts?
By making our confession to God, who comes bringing joy and
grace to all. Please join me as we pray.

Unison Prayer Of Confession
O promised Christ,
our world is torn by violence and death,
our peace depends on your coming.
We sin against others,
our forgiveness depends on your coming.
Full of good intentions, we are poor at keeping promises,
our only hope in being your people
is in your coming to transform our lives.
Lord Christ, flesh-bearing Word,
our world waits:
for your peace,
> **which comes as softly**
> **as a snowfall;**
for your mercy,
> **which fills the emptiness**
> **of our souls;**

for your grace,
   which is always more
   than our hearts can ever hold.
Immanuel, come quickly, we pray.

Silence is kept

Assurance Of Pardon

One: In this season of waiting, the good news is forgiveness of sins, the gift of Advent is new life. Let us commit our lives to Christ's way of peace and hope.

All: **Thanks be to the Advent God, who comes among us, setting us free to love and serve. Amen.**

Christmas Eve

Isaiah 9:2-7
Titus 2:11-14
Luke 2:1-14 (15-20)

Greeting

One: The people walking in darkness
have seen a great light;

**All: on those living in the shadows of death,
a light has dawned.**

One: Jesus Christ is our life and light.
In Christ's name, welcome!
In Christ's grace, let us worship God!

Call To Worship

One: Let us go, just as we are, to see what has happened.
Let us go with the shepherds,

**All: let us go and find the One
of whom the angels sang.**

One: Let us go with those who are wise,

**All: let us go and find the One
who brings God's truth to us.**

One: Let us go with the poor in spirit, and in flesh;
let us go with those who are humbled by life,

**All: let us find the Glory of God
born in a stable, and placed in a feeding trough.**

One: Let us go with our friends and family,
let us go with our neighbors and with strangers,
let us go with all the children of God,

**All: let us go to find the One who comes
to lead us home to God's kingdom.**

One: O come, let us go to the Babe of Bethlehem;
O come, let us adore him!

All: Christ our Lord!

Call To Reconciliation

We begin with such great hopes, such great dreams. We are going to be better, to treat others more fairly, and to love more deeply. But we come to the manger once again, knowing our failings, and aware of our brokenness. Let us confess to the One who comes, that our lives might be made new.

Unison Prayer Of Confession
God, who comes to us,
forgive us ...
    when our shadowed lives dim your Light,
    when the tinsel for Christmas means more
        than your truth;
    when our hearts of stone resist the pain
        and brokenness around us;
    when we care more about what is under
        the tree than the damage we do
        to your creation and to your children.
Have mercy on us, Healing God,
so we might
    tear down the walls we have built
        to keep your love away;
so we could
    seek your justice for our sisters and brothers;
so our hearts
    would become cradles for your Son,
    our Lord and Savior, Jesus Christ.

Silence is kept

Assurance Of Pardon (based on Isaiah 62:10-12)
One: Go, go through the city, preparing for the people;
        repair, repair all the roads, filling in the holes,
        raising a banner for all to see.
        God has spoken to all people,
        saying to sons and daughters:

"See your Savior comes;
to make good on my promises,
to bring redemption to all people."

All: **And we will be called God's Beloved,
the Redeemed of the Lord;
God will seek us out to live in the New Jerusalem,
where no one is left behind. Amen.**

Christmas Day

Isaiah 52:7-10
Hebrews 1:1-4 (5-12)
John 1:1-14

Call To Worship

One: Wonder of wonders,
      God has come to us!

**All: Not as a judge, but as a Savior;
        not in power, but as a servant.**

One: Wonder of wonders,
      God comes to us!

**All: Not in silence, but in the Word made flesh;
        not in the shadows, but bringing light.**

One: Wonder of wonders,

All: God is with us!

Prayer Of The Day

Angels sang their anthems
at the midnight hour
to awaken a sleeping creation;
shepherds came to worship you,
and went away rejoicing;
wise ones gave their hearts to you,
so they could dwell in yours.
O Immanuel,
we adore you!

You came to us as a baby
to hold us in your grace;
you came to us in a stable,
so we would have no trouble finding you;
you came to us in poverty,
to enrich our lives.

O Beautiful Messenger of Peace,
we adore you!
You play hopscotch with us
in the streets of the kingdom;
you build your home
deep within our souls;
you walk with us
in the winter of life.
O wisdom from on high,
we adore you!

God in Community, Holy in One,
all the faithful lift their songs of joy to you,
even as we pray, as Jesus has taught us,
> **Our Father ...**

Call To Reconciliation

God became one of us so we could see the face of love, hear the voice of peace, be touched by the hand of grace, and know the heart of mercy. God comes to us, offering us forgiveness and peace. Join with me as we pray together, saying,

Unison Prayer Of Confession

You came in weakness, Mighty God,
> **forgive our grasping**
> **for power.**

You came in humility, Prince of Peace,
> **forgive us**
> **when we applaud power.**

You came in poverty, Everlasting One,
> **forgive us**
> **when we do not see your family**
> **sleeping in our streets.**

You came in gentleness, Wonderful Counselor,
> **forgive us**
> **for the anger we speak**
> **and the pain we cause.**

Child of Bethlehem,
    forgive us,
    heal us,
    make us new;
    then we will join the angels in singing your praises
    this Christmas Day and all the days to come.

Silence is kept

Assurance Of Pardon

One: Break forth into song, children of God,
        for the Babe comes to comfort us;
        like a mother rocking her son to sleep,
        like a father wiping away the tears of his daughter.
All: *(sung)* **Joy to the world, the Lord is come,**
        Let earth receive her king.
        Let every heart, prepare him room.
        And heaven and nature sing,
        and heaven and nature sing,
        and heaven, and heaven and nature sing.

Christmas 1

Isaiah 63:7-9
Hebrews 2:10-18
Matthew 2:13-23

Call To Worship
One: All God's people — boys and girls, women and men,
All: come and worship!
One: Shepherds, Magi, saints, and angels,
All: come and worship!
Come and worship!
One: All who need the Savior, all who long for comfort,
All: come and worship!
Come and worship Christ,
the newborn King!

Prayer Of The Day
In your love, which never ends,
Steadfast God,
you hear the cries
of all the two-year-olds
cast aside by the world,
and the weeping of their mothers
who cannot feed them
because there is no hope.

Wrapped in an old blanket
to keep you warm in a cold stable,
and smuggled into Egypt
to keep you safe, Marginalized Messiah,
you know the searching of refugees
for a place they can call home,
for a life they can call free.

Cradling the innocents killed in war,
remembering those driven from their homes
by fear, or greed, or power,
singing laments with all the parents
who cannot give their children the lives
that they should have,
you proclaim God's name to us,
Spirit of Sanctuary.

God in Community, Holy in One,
you fill our hearts with joy,
for you continue to come into this world.
Give us the peace, the joy, the hope to carry
to all who cry out to you this day,
even as we pray as Jesus has taught us, saying,
Our Father ...

Call To Reconciliation

Born of Mary, in a child called Jesus, God knew life as we
know it: our pains, our doubts, our temptations, our hopes. Without sin, Jesus could choose to judge us; instead, he redeems us and
is the midwife of our birth into new life. Let us confess our sins, so
we might be filled with God's grace and joy in this season of holiness and hope.

Unison Prayer Of Confession

**Dweller in Eternity, you became a little baby for us. We
chase down the corridors of power, while you enter the hallways where weakness and suffering reside. We grab for more
and more, while you let go of glory to become one of us. We
reduce our Savior's birth to tinsel, toys, and trash to be placed
on the curb, while you widen your embrace to welcome all
thrown out by the world.**

**Forgive us, Joyous Love. Come among us, filling our
hearts with your grace and truth. Open our lips, so we might
sing with the angels. Send us forth with the shepherds, to tell**

27

everyone we meet the good news of the birth of the One who brings us life, Jesus Christ, our Lord and Savior.

Silence is kept

Assurance Of Pardon

One: The news we have hungered for fills our lives;
the news we have been searching for has found us;
the news that is for all people is proclaimed;
a Savior has been born, for us!

**All: The One who is our hope has arrived;
the One who is our life has come to us;
the One who is our joy is in our midst,
Jesus Christ the Lord! Thanks be to God. Amen.**

Christmas 2

Jeremiah 31:7-14
Ephesians 1:3-14
John 1:(1-9) 10-18

Call To Worship
One: On this day,
we remember the gift of God's Word
All: who gathers us together from the farthest parts of the
world to worship in joy and hope.
One: On this day,
we remember the gifts of bread and wine,
All: the simple gifts that are shaped
into God's nourishing grace.
One: On this day,
we remember the gifts of water and oil
All: cleansing us in the baptism pools,
anointing us as God's children.

Prayer Of The Day
You could let us continue to shuffle
through the world's deserts,
God of Christmas,
but you choose to walk with us
beside the rivers of life.
You could forget who we are,
but you adopt us into your family,
your children of hope and joy.
You could decide we are not worth all the love
and all the agony of caring,
but you redeem us and make us whole.
Blessed are you!

It was only the other day
the angels were singing of your birth, Tiny One of Bethlehem,

and now, here you are,
running swiftly toward us:
to melt our frozen faith,
to comfort us in our loneliness,
to lead us into life in your kingdom.
Blessed are you!

At the edge of a new year,
we wonder what life will be like,
and what do you do,
Gathering Spirit?

You water our parched souls with laughter;
you teach dance steps to those
too weary to tap their toes;
you fill our emptiness
with gladness!
Blessed are you!

God in Community, Holy in One,
we bless you, as we pray as Jesus teaches us, saying,
Our Father ...

Call To Reconciliation

Have we really been to Bethlehem? Have we worshiped at the manger? Have we changed, for the better? Or have we simply gone back to being the people we were before the joy, the peace, the gift of Christmas? Let us confess how we have not lived as those who have seen the Baby, as we pray together, saying,

Unison Prayer Of Confession
God of Christmas,
> **we still are playing with our new toys,**
> **the manger figures have not been put away,**
> **we still sing the Christmas carols,**
> **but we have gone back to our old ways.**
> **We set limits on who we will love.**
> **We make promises we cannot keep.**
> **We fail to see the pain and hurt we cause.**

God of the angels and shepherds, forgive us.
Your Word has come to reshape our lives;
your light has come to show us the way home;
your Son has come to make us your family.
Have mercy and make us new people.
In Jesus' name, we pray.

Silence is kept

Assurance Of Pardon

One: Like the Baby of Bethlehem, we are born anew. God's forgiveness cradles us; God's love is poured out upon us.

All: What a marvelous gift — forgiveness! Filled with hope and new life, we can sing God's praises forever. Amen.

The Epiphany Of Our Lord

Isaiah 60:1-6
Ephesians 3:1-12
Matthew 2:1-12

Call To Worship

One: He came as a baby,
   to bring laughter to children;

All: **he came for young adults home from college,**
   and for newborns at their mothers' breasts.

One: He was born in a stable,
   to bring hope to the poor;

All: **he came for those who have more than they need,**
   and for those who could give away more than they dare.

One: He was worshiped by shepherds,
   and gifted by kings;

All: **the Christ Child is born!**
   Let us follow the star to find him.

Prayer Of The Day

They waited until your star appeared
and then rushed to find you,
bringing expectant hearts,
rejoicing in the light that guided them,
hoping that all their dreams would come true.
We thank you for the waiting,
God of Advent.

They rejoiced in the simplicity of a stable,
when no homes were opened to them;
their hearts celebrated your birth
as the shepherds rejoiced at the manger;
they hoped their dreams
would come true.

We thank you for the joy,
Child of Christmas.

We are drawn to your light
like moths to a flame;
our emptiness is filled with your grace
as your glory shines in all nations;
we are led to the wonders of hope,
as the light of faith reveals the way.
We thank you for revealing the mystery,
Spirit of Epiphany.

God in Community, Holy in One,
we thank you for the gift of the star,
as we pray as Jesus teaches us, saying,
Our Father ...

Call To Reconciliation
The light has come, but we still seem to prefer the darkness of temptation and desire. Let us confess our sins to God, so the light will fill every shadow of our lives.

Unison Prayer Of Confession
In truth, God of Epiphany, we come to worship you, but our motives (like Herod's) are not pure. We want you to reward us because we are here, and not someplace else. We want you to gift us with health, with wealth, with answers to our questions. We want you to overlook our unfaithfulness, rather than shining the bright light of the Christ Child in our lives.

Forgive us, Star Shaper, that we are not more like those wise ones of so long ago. In following a star, they found hope; in gifting a child, they received grace; in seeking your signs, they discovered life. Be with us, in mercy and joy, as we journey with your Son, Jesus Christ, our Lord and Savior, in the season of light.

Silence is kept

Assurance Of Pardon

One: Come, stand up, on your feet! God's grace has dawned in our hearts, eternity's light shines in our souls.

All: The light of the world shines in our lives, delivering us from evil, gracing us with hope and joy. Thanks be to God. Amen.

The Baptism Of Our Lord
Epiphany 1
Ordinary Time 1

Isaiah 42:1-9
Acts 10:34-43
Matthew 3:13-17

Call To Worship

One: When the floods and storms of the world threaten
to overwhelm us,

All: **God's peace flows through us,
to calm our troubled lives.**

One: When the thunder of the culture's claims on us
deafens us to hope,

All: **God whispers to us
and soothes our souls.**

One: When the wilderness begs us to come out and play,

All: **God takes us by the hand
and we dance into the garden of grace.**

Prayer Of The Day

Your voice whispers
over the waters of life,
echoing in our hearts.
Your voice shatters
the chain of sin,
so we may skip into the kingdom.
Your voice shakes
the wilderness we travel through,
blessing us with your peace.
And we cry, "Glory!"
God of Love.

35

You would not let your love be broken,
and so we are made whole;
you rescue us from death's row,
and we will live with you.
You will bring justice
to all who are needy and poor,
so we wait for you.
And we cry, "Glory!"
Beloved of God.

As we touch the waters of baptism,
touch us with your cleansing grace;
as we are healed by your peace,
may we bind up the brokenhearted;
as we are liberated by your love
may we work to free all captives.
And we cry, "Glory!"
Spirit of love.
We cry, "Glory!"

God in Community, Holy in One,
even as we pray as we have been taught,
   Our Father ...

Call To Reconciliation

It makes no difference if you were sprinkled, washed, or immersed. In baptism, you were claimed as God's own, and gifted with the Holy Spirit. Let us remember the promises of mercy, even as we confess our unfaithfulness.

Unison Prayer Of Confession

Brooder of Water, you call us to make no distinctions between people, yet we persist in dividing folks by class or race or age or whatever. You want us to tell of what we have learned about Jesus, but only silence is heard by others. You encourage us to trust the new life you offer, but we cling firmly to our past.

Forgive us, Fountain of Faith. In baptism, you call us by name, and tell us how loved we are. Remind us of the promises made to heal, to forgive, and to transform us in the living waters of Jesus Christ, our Lord and Savior.

Silence is kept

Assurance Of Pardon

One: This is the good news! Baptized in water, we are God's beloved, forgiven and made whole by the grace that flows through us.

All: Thanks be to God! Filled with the Spirit, overflowing with hope, we will bear witness to all of what God has done in our lives. Amen.

Epiphany 2
Ordinary Time 2

Isaiah 49:1-7
1 Corinthians 1:1-9
John 1:29-42

Call To Worship
One: Gathered in winter's grayness,
      we wait,
All: **looking for the One**
      who is the light for all people.
One: Called to be saints,
      we wait,
All: **to listen to the One**
      who is not speechless
      when it comes to good news.
One: Commissioned to be servants,
      we wait,
All: **to be enriched with every spiritual gift,**
      so we can spend them on others.

Prayer Of The Day
Like a teacher,
Faithful God,
you bend down to listen
to our hearts;
like a friend,
you stretch your hand
to pull us out of the holes
we have dug for ourselves;
like a mother,
you teach us new songs
to hum throughout the day.

You carry salvation
to every corner of creation,
Tender Lamb,
so light might fill
our shadowed souls;
so our ears
might be opened
to stories of faithful saints;
so your strength
might carry us
when we are too weak to follow.

You are not speechless,
Wisdom's Word,
when we need stories of faithfulness;
you are not voiceless
when our hearts need new songs;
you are not silent
when the world is broken,
but call us to serve with you.

God in Community, Holy in One,
hear us as we lift the prayer Jesus taught us,
Our Father ...

Call To Reconciliation

In our impatience to have our own way, to have our every want and wish fulfilled, we pay little attention to God's will and dreams for us. But God remains patient, leaning over to listen to our prayers and to teach us the songs of salvation. Let us confess to the One who waits for us to speak.

Unison Prayer Of Confession

Called to be saints, Eternal Patience, we confess the lives we truly lead. Gifted with open ears, we listen to the sales pitches of the world, not to your whispers of grace. We delight in the temptations we are offered, while ignoring your hopes for us.

We walk the shadowed streets of sin, while the light of the king-dom beckons to us.

Lamb of God, who takes away the sin of the world, have mercy on us. Strengthen us so that we may become your dependable disciples, servants of the good news, tellers of stories of the love and hope you offer to a broken world in Jesus Christ, our Lord and Savior.

Silence is kept

Assurance Of Pardon

One: The good news is not kept hidden from us, but revealed in the gift of Jesus Christ. The One who calls us is also the One who forgives us.

All: Grant us your peace, loving God, and live with us for-ever. Amen.

Epiphany 3
Ordinary Time 3

Isaiah 9:1-4
1 Corinthians 1:10-18
Matthew 4:12-23

Call To Worship
One: You call us, O God,
          to have the same mind
All: **so we can know**
          each other's joys and sorrows.
One: You call us, O God,
          to have the same purpose
All: **so we can be one people**
          who are not afraid to follow Jesus.
One: You call us, O God,
          to have the same mission
All: **so we can serve together in your kingdom.**

Prayer Of The Day
You will not play
hide-and-seek with us,
Revealing God,
but you invite us to watch
with wide-open eyes
as you break our burdens
into manageable pieces;
as you take our tentative hope
and multiply it with abounding joy;
as you shelter us
in the storms of life.

You call us,
Teacher of Tenderness,

to make us gatherers
of all who are lost;
bearers of light
to those in despair's gloom;
storytellers of hope and grace
to the world's straining ears.

Speak to us,
Spirit of Foolish Grace,
so that we may know
that we are all one,
always and in every moment,
eager to follow you
into the wonder of your kingdom.

We lift our voices to sing
our praise to you,
God in Community, Holy in One,
even as we pray, saying,
Our Father ...

Call To Reconciliation

However we have hurt others, whatever wrong we have done, our hearts whisper to us to seek God's face, to walk into the light of salvation, and to embrace the healing grace of God's heart.

Unison Prayer Of Confession

We go through our lives, O God, arguing with our families and friends over foolish issues. You call us to follow you, and we dawdle in making up our minds whether or not to respond. You would shelter us in the comfort of your grace, but we take solace in the gloom of the world.

Forgive us, Light of our Lives. Continue to proclaim the good news of the life that has come to us in the gentle grace and healing hope of Jesus Christ, our Lord and Savior.

Silence is kept

Assurance Of Pardon

One: The message of salvation is this: Christ came proclaiming the good news of God's kingdom, teaching us to live with one another, healing our every brokenness.

All: **God has multiplied our joy, so that it overflows our hearts, to be a blessing and comfort to everyone we meet. Amen.**

Epiphany 4
Ordinary Time 4

Micah 6:1-8
1 Corinthians 1:18-31
Matthew 5:1-12

Call To Worship

One: We are blessed when we hunger for justice
           and thirst for righteousness.

All: **Our souls are filled with God's hope and grace.**

One: We are blessed when we grieve over
           the brokenness of the world,

All: **choosing, as God does, to be with those
        who are weak and powerless.**

One: We are blessed when we become God's fools,

All: **willing to do what is right;
        not what is easy to do.**

Prayer Of The Day

The hills sing of your hopes,
and the valleys echo your dreams,
Holy God,
of a world
where we catch sight of you
in the innocent hearts of children;
where we listen to the wisdom
of souls willing to be weak;
where we find the home we long for
in your heart's brokenness.

Teacher of our Hearts,
when we are generous to the poor,
your kingdom of justice is built;
when we love kindness
more than we do power,

we are heirs of creation's grace;
when we walk hand-in-hand
with the humble-hearted,
we are in step with you;
when we share a picnic of hope and joy
with the forgotten of the world,
we follow you up the hill of faithfulness.

Wisdom of Weakness,
when our differences with one another
become stumbling blocks to life together,
you come
with your hopeful foolishness
so your children
might be at peace,
and a blessing of life
to a world in need of healing.

God in Community, Holy in One,
hear us as we pray as Jesus has taught us, saying,
Our Father ...

Call To Reconciliation
Called to be weak,
    we idolize the powerful;
called to be foolish,
    we hunger for the world's wisdom;
called to be poor in spirit,
    we thirst for more and more.
Let us confess to God how following
Jesus is often a stumbling block for us.

Unison Prayer Of Confession
How do we approach you, Exalted God, with our confessions? We make you weary with our inability to do justice for the poor and outcast. We gossip about those who are close to us, instead of being their loving friend. We make promises, and then go back on our word.

Forgive us, God of Hope, and bless us with your mercy. By your peace, we can do justice; by your love, we can act kindly; by your grace, we can walk with you as humbly and hopefully as did our Lord and Savior, Jesus Christ.

Silence is kept

Assurance Of Pardon

One: It is through foolishness that God makes us wise;
it is through weakness that God strengthens us to serve;
it is through forgiveness that God makes us whole.

All: **We cannot boast in what we have done, but only in the grace and joy of our God, who showers us with mercy. Amen.**

Epiphany 5
Ordinary Time 5

Isaiah 58:1-9a (9b-12)
1 Corinthians 2:1-12 (13-16)
Matthew 5:13-20

Call To Worship

One: To a society that lives in the shadowed recesses
of doubt and fear,

All: God calls us to be light.

One: To a world where every appetite is fed
until there is no taste to life,

All: God calls us to be salt.

One: To a time when loyalties are discarded
as easily as the clothes we wear,

All: God calls us to be faithful.

Prayer Of The Day

Creator of the Day,
you rise before dawn
to make breakfast
for the poor,
to water our parched hearts
with the joy of grace,
and to patch the potholes
poverty has made
in the streets of the kingdom.

You proclaim
the mysteries of grace,
Voice of Fulfillment,
not with fancy words
but in weakness,
which gives strength
to the weary;

in compassion,
which offers the guest room
of your heart
to the homeless;
in love,
as you take off your coat,
and place it around the shoulders
of a shivering child.

You speak softly,
Revealer of Wonders,
using the alphabet blocks
of grace and hope,
so all can know
the hidden heart of God;
so all may know the words
to proclaim the Light
that has come into the world.

God in Community, Holy in One,
hear as we pray as faithful children,
   Our Father ...

Call To Reconciliation

It is so simple — make a sandwich for the hungry, open our ears to the crying child, and change unjust laws. These are how we are called to worship God. Let us confess how we have not answered this call as we pray, saying,

Unison Prayer Of Confession

We confess, Holy One, how in superstition, we will throw salt over our shoulders, but find it hard to flavor a world made bland by the ordinary. We dim our gifts to save our energy, instead of shining as long as we can in society's shadowed corners. We skip a meal once a week to show our faith, but are unable to see those who go through the dumpster to feed their children.

Forgive us, and have mercy, Creation's Goodness. By your grace, heal our brokenness, so we might fix the shattered dreams of our world; with your hope, strengthen our hearts, so we might fill the emptiness of our society. This we ask in the wonderful name of Jesus Christ, our Lord and Savior.

Silence is kept

Assurance Of Pardon

One: God has heard our prayers and come to us to sweeten our bitterness with hope — to shatter our darkness with the light of mercy.

All: **We will share this good news without being ordered to; we will praise God's name because we want to. Thanks be to God. Amen.**

Epiphany 6
Ordinary Time 6

Deuteronomy 30:15-20
1 Corinthians 3:1-9
Matthew 5:21-37

Call To Worship
One: You could have stayed in bed,
         you could be eating breakfast out.
All: **We have chosen to be in this place,**
         feasting on God's word.
One: You could give a cold shoulder to your neighbors,
         you could warm yourself in front of the fireplace.
All: **We have chosen to see God**
         with more than just a sliver of our hearts.
One: You could be chasing after the world's idols,
         you could be listening to television's talking heads.
All: **We have chosen to serve the One**
         who blesses us with life.

Prayer Of The Day
Mothering God,
you nurse us with the milk
of blessing and joy,
so we may grow in faith
to feast on grace and hope;
you plow the fields of our hearts,
planting the seeds of love,
so we may be your people.
We hold fast to you,
God of Choices.

You provide the road map
for our journey,
so we will not wander down blame's alleys.

When we choose sides
by our quarreling and cliques,
you reconcile us
to each other
with your words.
We hold fast to you,
Jesus of Reconciliation.

Blessed with the fresh breeze
of your presence and power,
we will continue to follow you,
trusting that you will lead us
into making right choices
as the disciples of Jesus.
We hold fast to you,
Transforming Spirit.

God in Community, Holy in One,
we hold fast to you, even as we pray
as Jesus has taught us,
    Our Father ...

Call To Reconciliation

Following God is not like flipping a coin. It is intentional; it is difficult; it is risky. That is why we know all the ways we have failed in our discipleship and need to come to God. We choose to confess, so we might embrace the forgiveness God offers to us.

Unison Prayer Of Confession

Invited to walk in your footsteps, Wanderer of the Universe, we turn away to play hopscotch on the sidewalks of seduction. Given the chance to watch you work wonders of grace and renewal, we fixate on the idols of success and power. When you want to tell us stories of healing and reconciliation, we decline to hear your gentle voice.

Have mercy on us, God of Blessings, and help us to choose to hold fast to your hand; to walk your streets of wholeness and

51

hope; to follow our Lord and Savior, Jesus Christ, into the life you intend for us.

Silence is kept

Assurance Of Pardon
One: God's forgiveness dwells in our hearts; Christ's love fills us; the Spirit's peace guides our steps.

All: Our feet are set on the journey. We walk in faith and hope with our God. Amen.

Epiphany 7
Ordinary Time 7

Leviticus 19:1-2, 9-18
1 Corinthians 3:10-11, 16-23
Matthew 5:38-48

Call To Worship
One: God would teach us to love,
      even the imperfect people,
**All: so we can love others
      as we love ourselves.**
One: God would teach us to deny ourselves,
      even walking the extra mile with us,
**All: so we can give ourselves to others
      as generously as Christ has been given to us.**
One: God would teach us new ways
      to journey through life,
**All: so we can follow the footprints of the Word
      all the way to the kingdom.**

Prayer Of The Day
When we see you sharing your hope
with the poor, the immigrant, the stranger;
when we watch you build a ramp
for those in wheelchairs;
when we experience your willingness
to help us in spite of our stubbornness;
when we hear your call to love
over our yearnings to hate;
we know what holiness looks like,
God of Creation.

When you refuse to speak harshly
to those who judge you;

when you wipe away the tears
of those who would hurt you;
when you choose to respond nonviolently
to those who would crucify you;
we know what peace looks like,
Light of the World.

When we hear you whisper
of fairness and justice;
when you fill our hands with grace
to be shared with others;
when you build our lives
on the foundation of Christ's peace and love;
we know what power looks like,
Spirit alive in us.
We know what you look like,

God in Community, Holy in One,
and so we pray as Jesus has taught us,
even as we yearn to be your image here on earth,
Our Father ...

Call To Reconciliation

God would teach us all we need: to live in peace, to love others, to walk the right paths. Let us confess how foolish we are not to listen to such wisdom, as we pray together, saying,

Unison Prayer Of Confession
A friends hurts us,
we hurt back;
someone hits us,
we strike back;
a family member ridicules us,
we gossip about him or her.
That's how we have been taught to deal
with those around us.

But now, God of Mercy,
you call us to a different life:
    the lift of forgiving, not revenge;
    the life of peace, not anger;
    the life of love, not hate.
As you forgive us of all we have done,
may we walk in your new ways of living,
as we follow Jesus, our Lord, our Savior, our Teacher.

Silence is kept

Assurance Of Pardon

One: It begins with God and ends with God — that love can create, renew, restore. God loves you and forgives you — now and forever.

All: **As we listen to God's songs of mercy, we are cradled in grace — now and forever. Amen.**

Epiphany 8
Ordinary Time 8

Isaiah 49:8-16a
1 Corinthians 4:1-5
Matthew 6:24-34

Call To Worship

One: When our hearts are so heavy
it seems we cannot carry them through the day,

All: **God will give us compassion through our friends
so we do not bear the load alone.**

One: When our words are so inadequate
it seems we cannot speak them,

All: **God will give us hope
so we can break forth in songs of joy.**

One: When we have so lost our way
we stumble in the shadows of life,

All: **God will give us light,
so we can find the living waters.**

Prayer Of The Day

To those who hunger and thirst
in the loneliness of life,
you nourish them with compassion;
to those who huddle
in the shadows of unhappiness,
you bring the light of joy.
You love us like a mother, Holy God.

To those held captive
by the stress of daily living,
you whisper, "Let go; cling to me."
To those who wonder each morning
what they should wear to school,

you hand a bouquet of daisies.
You watch over us like a father, Jesus of our Hearts.

For those who stumble through life,
you fill in the potholes of their worries;
for all those forgotten
by all rushing by them,
you tattoo our faces on your palms,
so you will see us
every time you pray for us.
Like our parents,
you remember us, Spirit of Joy.

God in Community, Holy in One,
hear us as we pray as we have been taught,
Our Father ...

Call To Reconciliation

Called to be servants and stewards of mysteries, we worry more about how others will judge our hairstyles or choice of shows. Let us go to God's store, where we will find grace and mercy, before wasting our blessings on the trinkets of the world.

Unison Prayer Of Confession
You tell us not to worry, Mothering God,
but we cannot seem to help ourselves.
With refrigerators full of food,
we still make grocery lists;
with closets so full we cannot shut the doors,
we run and buy new outfits;
for a simple invitation to "Follow me,"
we form committees to help us decide.

We lift our hearts to you, Tender God, so you would fill them with your mercy and hope. May we continue to seek your kingdom in every moment to come, hoping and trusting in the peace and love of Jesus Christ, our Lord and Savior.

Silence is kept

Assurance Of Pardon

One: Like a nursing child fed by its mother, God's mercy calms and quiets us, so we can receive all that God wants to give to us.

All: We welcome all that God gives to us, and will share these gifts with everyone we meet. Amen.

Epiphany 9
Ordinary Time 9

Deuteronomy 11:18-21, 26-28
Romans 1:16-17; 3:22b-28 (29-31)
Matthew 7:21-29

Call To Worship
One: Here is the promise:
        When you ask for help, God will respond.
All: **We will put these words in our hearts.**
One: Here is the promise:
        God's salvation is for all, a gift of grace.
All: **We will share these words with our children.**
One: Here is the promise:
        Whether we are foolish or wise, God loves us all.
All: **We will carry these words with us through life.**

Prayer Of The Day
When we get trapped
in the shifting sands of prejudice,
you build fairness as a model for us;
when we stumble over the marginalized
sinking in their oppression,
you build justice into our hearts;
when we would choose the easy way
of cursing others and ourselves,
you whisper blessings into our souls.
Holy are you, God of Creation.

When we have no words to offer
to all those who suffer,
you write compassion on our hearts,
so we may serve them.

When we wonder what we can say
to our children as they ponder
a future they cannot see,
you write hope onto our hearts,   .
so we may teach them.
Holy are you, Friend of the Forgotten.

When we think that only fools
would believe in this thing called the gospel,
you wisely give us mentors
to show us the way.
When we think we have earned
enough bonus points to get into heaven,
you wisely remind us
that it is what God has done for us
that makes all the difference.
Holy are you, Spirit of Joy.

Holy, holy, holy are you,
God in Community,
and we lift the prayer Jesus has taught us, saying,
  Our Father ...

Call To Reconciliation

Each moment, and every moment; each day and every day, we face choices. Will we help, or hurt another; will we speak in anger or love; will we see God in the other, or ignore them all together? Let us confess to God the poor choices we have made in our lives, as we pray, saying,

Unison Prayer Of Confession

Why do we worry so much about earning points with you, Heart of Holiness, when it is your grace that sets us free? Why is it we can glide so gracefully through temptation, yet trip when we try to follow Jesus? Why do the false promises of the world tantalize our souls, while we cannot remember your words of blessing?

Forgive us, Foundation of Faith, when we make the wrong choices. Write your words of grace and hope on the doors of our hearts, so we can open them to the love and mercy Jesus Christ, our Lord and Savior, brings to us.

Silence is kept

Assurance Of Pardon

One: It is not because of anything we do, or by some great human endeavor on our part, that God forgives us. It is finally, and simply, because of God's gracious love for us.

All: **Now, we stand on solid ground; now, we find our sins forgiven; now, we find our shattered lives put back together. Thanks be to God. Amen.**

The Transfiguration Of Our Lord (Last Sunday After Epiphany)

Exodus 24:12-18
2 Peter 1:16-21
Matthew 17:1-9

Call To Worship
One: We gather as the faithful of God,
       we come to listen to what God has to say to us.
All: **God has invited us to this place;**
       may our faces reflect our hopes and our hearts.
One: We gather as the faithful of God,
       people of the new covenant of hope and promise.
All: **We boldly enter into the presence of God,**
       hoping to be transformed into new people.
One: We gather as the faithful of God,
       our fears melting away in the heart of God.
All: **We come to share in the freedom of the Spirit,**
       we come to praise God's holy name.

Prayer Of The Day
Majestic Glory,
Heart of God,
on mountaintops crowned with mist
and in museums filled with wonder
in tents pitched by singing brooks
and in theaters filled with laughing children,
in this sacred space
and in all the ordinary neighborhoods where we live,
you are with us,
hearing us,
answering us,
and we do not lose heart.

Holy Beloved,
Face of God,
we glance at you
out of the corners of our souls
and see grace surrounding us;
we look at you conversing with the poor and rejected,
and see our families;
we watch you as you come to us,
to touch us, to heal us,
and to give us back to God —
and we do not lose heart.

Holy Spirit,
Ear of God,
when our lips
cannot shape words
you speak them for us;
when we can only sigh
our needs,
you gather them up
and offer them to God;
when our hopes are dashed to the ground,
you pick them up
and give them back to us —
and we do not lose heart.

God in Community, Holy in One,
we lift our voices and hearts to you,
praying as Jesus taught us, saying,
> **Our Father ...**

Call To Reconciliation

Sometimes it seems that we wait for God to astound us with mighty wonders, while God knows that what we need is grace. God waits to forgive us, so let us hold nothing back, but trust in the One who listens to our prayers and answers us with mercy.

Unison Prayer Of Confession

God of Mountaintops, the din of the world can harden our hearts to your word. We watch news, reality television, silly sitcoms, and yet have trouble bearing witness to your presence in our lives. Our faith is placed in those who fail us, our trust is given to those who misplace it.

Forgive us, Revealer of Mystery. You offer mercy to us, that we might hear your call to discipleship. You whisper our names, that we might know how loved we are. Caught by the surprise of your never-ending love for us, how can we not follow our Lord and Savior, Jesus Christ, onto the mountaintops of worship and into the valleys of sacrifice and service?

Silence is kept

Assurance Of Pardon

One: On mountaintops and in the valleys, in our homes and in our hearts, God knows us better than we know ourselves, and God forgives us when we cannot forgive ourselves.

All: **By God's mercy, we are forgiven.**
By God's mercy, we are made whole.
By God's mercy, we are equipped to serve others.
Thanks be to God. Amen.

Ash Wednesday

Joel 2:1-2, 12-17
Psalm 51
2 Corinthians 5:20b—6:10
Matthew 6:1-6, 16-21

*(**Note:** We use Taizé songs for our worship, but other songs can be substituted for other congregations.)*

Silent Prayer In Preparation For Worship
As you begin this service, take a few moments to bring yourself before God — your present state of mind and preoccupations, as well as your desire to meet God during this time.

Call To Worship
One: God's people have been called to gather.
**All: From breast-feeding infants to aged grandparents,
all are welcome.**
One: God's people have been called to repent.
**All: From those who wear their faults on their sleeves
to those whose secret hearts are broken,
all are welcome.**
One: God's people have been called to be reconciled to our God.
**All: From those who have turned away,
to those whose pain whispers in the night,
all are welcome.**

Taizé Song, "Wait For The Lord"

Prayer Of The Day
God of Holiness,
your day comes near
and we tremble,
not out of fear,

but from awe and gratitude.
For on your day,
we are fully known,
completely restored,
reconciled to you forever.

Jesus Christ,
Grace Bearer,
as we come to your fast,
may we be filled with your hope;
as we receive your gifts,
may our hearts be opened to others;
as we begin our journey with you,
may we put no roadblocks
in the path to Jerusalem.

Holy Spirit,
Creator of Clean Hearts,
as water rushes into an empty hole,
may your sacramental silence fill the emptiness of our souls.

God in Community, Holy in One,
our Treasure, our Hope, our Joy,
hear us as we pray as Jesus taught us, saying,
   Our Father ...

Taizé Song, "In The Lord, I'll Be Ever Thankful"

Read Joel 2:1-2, 12-17

Taizé Song, "Our Darkness"

Psalm 51 *(read in unison)*

Taizé Song, "In God Alone My Soul"

Read 2 Corinthians 5:20b—6:10

Taizé Song, "Our Eyes"

Read Matthew 6:1-6, 16-21

Silence is observed (ten minutes)

Invitation To Lenten Disciplines
Beloved in Christ,
at the time of the Christian Passover,
we celebrate our deliverance from sin and death
through the death and resurrection
of our Lord Jesus Christ.

Lent is the season of preparation
for this great celebration,
the means by which we renew our lives
in the Paschal mystery.

We begin our Lenten journey
by acknowledging our need for repentance,
for in penitence,
we name those things
that damage us and others
for what they really are,
and we open ourselves
to the One whose love knows no boundaries
and whose mercy is demonstrated to us
in the life of Jesus Christ.

By taking an honest look at our lives,
and repenting of our humanness;
by praying quietly,
but with full hearts;
by letting go of those things that harm us
and by taking on works of love for others;
by reading and feasting on God's word,
we observe a holy Lent,

and prepare ourselves for the passion of Holy Week
and the joy of Easter.
Let us prepare ourselves to come to our God.

Taizé Song, "O Lord, Hear My Prayer"

Call To Reconciliation
God begs us to turn from those words, those acts, and those
obstacles that keep us from being God's people. As we begin our
Lenten journey, I invite you to join with me, with words and in
silence, as we bring our brokenness to God who desires to make us
whole.

Unison Prayer Of Confession
**Too long we have traveled our own ways, Approaching
God, too long we have sought to satisfy our hidden desires.
We have trusted the falsehoods of the world, and relied on the
power that would consume our souls. We have sought healing
from imposters, and rejected the One who was broken for
our wholeness.**

**Have mercy on us, God whose love overflows our deepest
hopes. Let our hearts be a sanctuary for your Spirit; let our
lives abound in service to others; let our spirits reflect the One
we call our Lord and Savior, Jesus Christ. Amen.**

Silence is kept

Assurance Of Pardon
One: God lets go of the punishment we deserve and gives us
       mercy in its place. Willingly, God puts a new spirit into us,
       the spirit of hope and joy.
All: **We will sing to the One who has delivered us from our
       sins. We will praise God with cleansed hearts. Thanks
       be to God. Amen.**

68

Imposition Of The Ashes
Our ancestors in the faith
used ashes as a sign of our repentance,
a symbol of the uncertainty
and fragility of human life.
Like them,
we have tasted the ashes of hopelessness;
we have walked through the ashes of our loss and pain;
we have stood knee-deep in the ashes of our brokenness.
God of our Lives,
out of the dust of creation
you have formed us and given us life.
May these ashes not only be a sign,
of our repentance and death,
but reminders that by your gift of grace
in Jesus Christ, our Redeemer,
we are granted life forever with you. Amen.

(A period of silence will follow. Those who wish to do so, may come forward to have the sign of the cross placed on their foreheads or hands. The ashes are from palm branches used at Palm Sunday services in the past, mixed with oil.)

Invitation To The Table *(from Isaiah 58)*

Great Prayer Of Thanksgiving
One: People of God, the Lord be with you.
All: And also with you.
One: People of dust, lift up your hearts to God.
All: We lift them up to the One who created us.
One: People of ashes, give thanks to the Lord our God.
**All: Praise and thanks are offered to the One
            who restores us to life.**

Now is the right time to praise you;
now is the moment to sing your praises,
Holy God of Creation.

You formed us to live in joy
and peace with you,
but we tore your heart
when we chose our desires
over your dreams for us.
We prefer to swim in the cesspool of the world
rather than to be cleansed in your living waters.
We hunger more for the adulation of others than
for the quiet intimacy of your grace.
Yet, you did not turn away from us,
but remained true to your covenant,
calling us to return in the words
trumpeted by the prophets;
inviting us to gather in your kingdom,
entreating us to accept your overflowing love.
Therefore, we glorify you,
joining our voices with those
who had wandered far from you,
but who were brought home;
and with those who seek you now
in this time and place.

Taizé Song, "Bless The Lord"

Holy are you, Steadfast Love,
and blessed is Jesus Christ,
Bread of Life.
Considered a pretender to David's throne,
he is your heart's true Son.
Taking on the poverty of the human spirit,
he shared the abundance of your heart;
weeping over our broken relationships,
he reconciles us with your saving joy;
having nothing he could call his own,
he gives us more than we ever need;
dying like a common criminal,

70

he gives us life,
releasing us from the grip of sin and death.
Preparing to journey with him once again,
we remember the mystery
of his faithful obedience to your heart.

Taizé Song, "Jesus Christ, Bread Of Life"

Holy Spirit, Heart of Compassion,
as the ashes of our humanity
are placed upon your baptismal seal,
so the brokenness of our lives
is placed on the table of grace,
that the bread might make us whole,
and the cup might fill us with hope.
Then, in your wisdom,
may we turn to serve others;
in your joy,
may we bear the burdens of others;
in your grace,
may our love overflow to others.
Through Christ, with Christ, in Christ,
in the community of the Holy Spirit,
all glory and honor are yours,
God of Holiness,
now and forever. Amen.

The Breaking Of The Bread And The Sharing Of The Cup

Taizé Song, "Eat This Bread"
   (Sing this as you receive communion)

Prayers Of Petition

Taizé Song, "Jesus Remember Me"

Please depart the sanctuary in silence.

Lent 1

Genesis 2:15-17; 3:1-7
Romans 5:12-19
Matthew 4:1-11

Litany For Lent

One: O Christ,
            as you head to Jerusalem,
            you lead us
            from the culture of selfishness
            into the kingdom of service;
            from our focus on fulfillment
            into acts of radical obedience;
            from a desire for esteem and honor
            into a life of self-denial.

All: **Save us, Lord Jesus.**

One: O Christ, Bearer of Mercy,
            you set down your glory
            to pick up the pieces of our broken lives
            and restore us as God's children.

All: **Save us, Brother Jesus.**

One: O Christ, Fullness of Grace,
            you emptied yourself
            so we might be filled
            with the power of the Holy Spirit.

All: **Save us, Bread of the World.**

One: O Christ, Breaker of Crafty Death,
            you are our hope in every moment,
            you are the promise of God's presence,
            you are the One who calls us to worship.

All: **Save us, Word of God.**

One: Jesus Christ, Lamb of God,

All: **have mercy on us.**

One: Lamb of God, who takes away all sin,
All: fill us with your hope.
One: Jesus Christ, Gift of Grace,
All: grant us your peace.
Silence
One: Creator God of all Love,
in Jesus Christ you have given us your very heart,
and so we offer ourselves to you,
seeking to follow Jesus in the way
he would lead us.
We would humbly do your will,
speaking your truth to all,
as you whisper your soul to us;
giving our lives in service to all,
as you fill us with the Holy Spirit;
walking the streets of the kingdom,
even as we pray the prayer
Jesus has taught us, saying,
All: Our Father ...

Call To Reconciliation

Like children, God sets boundaries for us that will lead us into goodness. Like children, we are stubborn enough to try to live our own way. We become easy prey for the evil one. But Jesus, who trusted and believed in God, helps us to find the will and strength to resist, and to experience the mercy of God. Together, let us confess our sins, that God would fill us with grace and hope.

Unison Prayer Of Confession

We confess, Eden's God, that Lent can make us very uncomfortable. We live in a culture that invites us to worship success, and you call us to sacrifice. We desire power, and you invite us to penitence and denial. We dwell in a "feel-good" society, and you ask us to become aware of the sufferings of our sisters, of the brokenness of our brothers.

By your mercy, restore us, God of Hope. As we walk toward Jerusalem with Jesus, may we walk toward your truth. As we

73

hear the hard words of sacrifice, may we hear the Spirit helping us to say, "No," to all that would distract us from discipleship. As we witness the suffering of our Lord, may we speak Christ's good news to all who are without hope and life in our world.

Silence is kept

Assurance Of Pardon

One: Left on our own, we would let our sins, our rebellion, and our obedience to God control our lives, but we have been given the gift of Jesus Christ.

All: **This is good news: The gift is freely given. The gift brings us grace. The gift brings us forgiveness. The gift brings us new life and peace with God and with one another. Thanks be to God for such a gift. Amen.**

Lent 2

Genesis 12:1-4a
Romans 4:1-5, 13-17
John 3:1-17

Call To Worship
One: Like Abraham and Sarah,
God calls us out of our comfort zones to new adventures.
All: In this season of discipleship,
may we respond with the trust and faith they model.
One: Like Nicodemus, we seek answers for our questions
from Jesus, especially the ones that awaken us at night.
All: In this season of questioning Jesus,
may we commit ourselves to listening
to what he has to say to us.
One: Like Paul, we affirm that our faith
is based on what God does for us,
not on our successes or failures.
All: In this season of self-denial,
may we give up our needs to save ourselves.
One: Like Abraham, Sarah, Nicodemus, Paul,
and all the others who have been our mentors in the faith,
All: we would follow God faithfully,
so our lives might be examples to those around us.

Prayer Of The Day
Creator of every moment,
Keeper of our every day,
take us by the hand and lead us,
as we trust you to walk with us
on the journey of life.

Watcher of our nights
and Answerer of our questions,
sweep away the cobwebs of our minds,

so we might discover anew
the promises you bring to us
in the word you plant within us.

Spirit of New Birth,
Breath of New Life,
be in the words we speak,
and sing, and pray
in this time of worship.
Reshape us into the people of God
created for worship and for service.

God in Community, Holy in One,
hear us as we pray as Jesus taught us, saying,
   Our Father ...

Call To Reconciliation

In the quiet moments, late in the day, in the middle of the night, we know ourselves for who we are and how we have failed to listen to God and be led where God would send us. And, in such moments, God waits to hear our confession and to forgive us, to make us new people, to help us be reborn as people of faith. Let us come to our God in trust.

Unison Prayer Of Confession

Because we are human, God of Faith, we believe we have nothing to learn from others, and so we ignore the lives of our ancestors like Sarah and Nicodemus. Because we are so wise, we look for answers to our questions in books, in food, in money, and in power, rather than to the One who knows the deepest longings of our hearts. Because we know all the answers, we have no need to change our way of living. We do not know where to find help when we are desperate.

Forgive us, Life-Keeping God. You are the One who can change our lives; you are the One who can transform our despair into hope; you are the One who can instill new life in us. We trust the promises that you will do this for us and open

our hearts, and our lives to your Son, Jesus Christ, our Lord and Savior.

Silence is kept

Assurance Of Pardon

One: God is our hope, our help, our peace, and our joy. God makes us new and sends us forth to be a blessing to all people.

All: **May we draw nearer to the Keeper of our Souls; to the Watcher of our days and nights; to the Spirit of new life and new hope — to the God who has forgiven us. Amen.**

Lent 3

Exodus 17:1-7
Romans 5:1-11
John 4:5-42

Call To Worship

One: We come, our souls thirsting for God,
      our spirits longing for love.
All: **We come to the One who supplies every need;**
      we come to the One who gives us living water.
One: We come, with prayers in our hearts,
      and with words too painful to speak.
All: **We come to the One who listens to our hearts,**
      who carries our suffering through eternity.
One: We come, with our brokenness and loss,
      with our hopes to be made whole.
All: **We come to the One who knows all our secrets,**
      who brings peace to all of us — and each of us.

Prayer Of The Day

You gathered up the earth,
shaping the mountains to awe us;
you filled the empty bowls
with living water,
so dolphins and little children
could swim in your joy.
You are our God,
and we worship you in joy.

We wander the deserts of our lives,
convinced that the wells of the world
will only fill our buckets
with lost hopes and dusty promises,
but you surprise us
with your questions and your answers,

letting us drink our fill
from the waters of life.
You are our Savior,
and we worship you in truth.

You saturate our arid souls
with your peace;
you fill disappointments
with your hope;
you take our broken hearts and make us one with God.
You are our comforter, and we worship you in spirit.

We worship you in spirit and truth,
God in Community, Holy in One,
even as we pray as we have been taught,
    Our Father ...

Call To Reconciliation

At a well drawing water, at a desk shuffling papers, at a stove cooking a meal — wherever we are, God meets us. To listen to our stories, to heal our brokenness, to forgive our sins, and to give us new life. Let us bring our prayers to the One who comes to us.

Unison Prayer Of Confession

Everlasting God, you know us better than we know ourselves. You hear the bitter words we speak to one another; you see the hurts we cause to those we claim to love; you bear the pain we inflict on everyone around us.

Fountain of Grace, in Jesus Christ you do not turn your back on sinners, but meet us where we are. Parched by the heat of our desires, you cool us with living water. Burdened by our failures, you shoulder them with us. Thirsting for hope in our lives, you send us our Lord and Savior, Jesus Christ.

Silence is kept

Assurance Of Pardon

One: Not when we had gotten it all right, but when we had gone wrong; not when we knew all the rules, but when we had broken God's heart — that's when Christ died for us, so we might live.

All: **What good news! What great joy! What wonderful hope! In Christ we are forgiven. Glory, God, glory! Amen.**

Lent 4

1 Samuel 16:1-13
Ephesians 5:8-14
John 9:1-41

Call To Worship
One: Here, in this place, with these people
All: **we find the One**
          who leads us into God's kingdom;
One: here, in God's kingdom,
          with our sisters and brothers in Christ,
All: **we find a feast**
          prepared for us;
One: here, in God's sanctuary,
          at this table of grace
All: **we eat of the goodness that heals us,**
          we drink of the mercy that is God's gift.

Prayer Of The Day
Shepherding God,
you create life
from the mud of the earth;
you draw forth light
from the shadowed corners of chaos;
your goodness and mercy
are our closest friends.
Great is your name.

Jesus, our Shepherd,
you open eyes
shuttered by sin and prejudice;
you heal lives shattered by bitterness;
you create pools of still grace in our stress-filled hearts.
Great is your love.

81

Holy Spirit, our Shepherd
through every darkened valley,
you plant seeds of goodness and mercy
deep within our souls,
so we would bear fruit for others;
you awaken us from our troubled sleep,
so we might be a light to the world.
Great is your peace.

God in Community, Holy in One,
hear us as we pray as Jesus has taught us, saying,
Our Father ...

Call To Reconciliation

How quick we are to notice the mistakes of others; yet never see our own faults! Before we judge other people, we need to pray that our blindness might be healed by God's gracious love. Please join me as we pray together, saying,

Unison Prayer Of Confession

God, our Great Shepherd, it is easy to lose sight of your kingdom, and your way for us. We hope that love conquers hate, that light shines in our shadows, that life is stronger than death — yet our lips are filled with bitter words, our lives are weak and shallow, the darkened corners of the world beckon to us.

Have mercy on us and lead us to the still waters of your grace and the healing garden of your heart, Tender Shepherd. Restore our sight to see you living with us; restore our hope so we might trust you; restore our speech so we might praise your great gift to us in Jesus Christ, our Lord and Savior.

Silence is kept

Assurance Of Pardon

One: With a gentle touch, with the anointing of the Holy Spirit, with the joy of love, God reaches out to forgive us and make us whole.

All: **Touch us, Eternal Spirit;**
heal us, Light of Love;
fill our lives with new meaning, God of Joy,
as we receive your forgiveness and grace. Amen.

Lent 5

Ezekiel 37:1-14
Romans 8:6-11
John 11:1-45

Call To Worship

One: Here, we gather to worship God;
here, we come to gather up hope.

All: **Here, we come to find renewed strength,
to put flesh on our faith.**

One: Here, we wait for God to speak;
here, God waits to fill our hearts.

All: **Here, we are reminded of God dwelling in us;
here, we encounter the One
who wipes away our tears.**

One: Here, we bring our pain and loneliness to God;
here, we seek the constant love of our God.

All: **Here, we are cradled by the One who weeps with us;
here, we are given the hope for which we long.**

Prayer Of The Day

Holy God,
Creator of Life,
in our darkened valleys,
you bring light;
in our crumbling communities,
you build your kingdom;
our barren lives are renewed
by your love.

Jesus Christ,
Mourner of the Dead,
by your tears
you take away our pain;

with your voice,
you call us to new life;
through your death,
you shatter all our fears of dying.

Holy Spirit,
Breath of God,
you live in every corner
of our souls;
you bind us to God
with your loving presence;
you breathe God's peace
into our sin-torn lives.

God in Community, Holy in One,
hear our hearts as we pray together, saying,
   Our Father ...

Call To Reconciliation

If God is keeping a record of our sins, we hope it will never be published. But, in reality, if the book was opened, every page would be blank, for God forgives us. Let us wait for God's mercy and grace, as we come to our God with our confession.

Unison Prayer Of Confession

Set free by your saving grace, Generous God, we confess that we are still confined by our pride and arrogance. We cannot throw off the grave clothes of habitual sin. We cling to our sins and fears, simply because they are so familiar and comfortable.

Yet, into every corner of our lives, into every shadow we fear, into death's dark tomb, you enter, Steadfast God. You break the bonds of sin and death, and call us to new life through the love and sacrifice of your Son, Jesus Christ, our Lord and Savior.

Silence is kept

85

Assurance Of Pardon

One: People of God, put your hope in God,
          for God offers us love that never fails,
          life that never ends.

All: **We wait for God, and God does not show up late.
          God's hope, God's love, God's grace are forever.
          Thanks be to God. Amen.**

Passion/Palm Sunday
(Lent 6)

Isaiah 50:4-9a
Philippians 2:5-11
Matthew 26:14—27:66 or Matthew 27:11-54

Call To Worship

One: Here, in this place,
           we prepare ourselves for the holiest of weeks.

All: **A week that ends one journey and begins another;**
           a week of heartache and loss,
           with hope hidden in hearts.

One: We will try to follow Jesus through this week,
           just as we have followed him to this day.

All: **We will wave our palm branches in joy;**
           we will clutch nails in our hands
           hidden behind our backs.

One: When he could have come with armies behind him,
           Jesus comes humbly,
           with children playing in the streets.

All: **Hosanna! Hosanna!**
           Blessed is the One who comes
           bringing the kingdom of God.

Prayer Of The Day

God of Hopes and Joys,
when our hearts ache from brokenness,
you nourish us with your love;
when the world's pain fatigues us,
you carry us in your arms;
when the loneliness of our souls
drains our very being,
you come and live with us.
You are our God.

Jesus Christ, God's True Son,
you did not profit
from your oneness with God,
but emptied yourself
to become servant to all humanity.
You humbled yourself
to lift us out of sin's grave.
You are our Lord.

Holy Spirit, Teacher from God,
humble us to be obedient,
even to the point of denying
all that keeps us from following Jesus;
teach us the words we need
to confess him as our Lord and Savior.
You are our helper.

God in Community, Holy in One,
we lift our prayers to you as Jesus has taught us, saying,
Our Father ...

Call To Reconciliation

One day, we are crying to God, "Save us," the next we are turning our backs on God and walking away. Despite our fickle nature, God is steadfast in loving us and constant in forgiving us. Let us confess to our God, as we pray,

Unison Prayer Of Confession

With joy in our hearts, we welcome your servant, O God, only to reject him when he picks up a cross instead of a crown. Like cloaks laid on the ground before Jesus, we pick up our faith, dust it off, and put it back in the closet until we need it. We can be as stubborn and rebellious as the city that cheers your name.

Save us, Redeeming God, save us! May we lay our doubts, our fears, our worries, and our weariness at your feet, trusting and believing that you will forgive what is sinful, make whole

our brokenness, and welcome us as sisters and brothers of our Lord and Savior, Jesus Christ.

Silence is kept

Assurance Of Pardon

One: Hosanna to David's Son! Blessed is the One who comes in God's name, not to judge us, but to save us.

All: We humble ourselves in gratitude to God, and in service to others, even as Christ did. Hosanna in the highest. Amen.

Maundy Thursday

Exodus 12:1-4 (5-10) 11-14
1 Corinthians 11:23-26
John 13:1-17, 31b-35

Call To Worship

One: In remembrance, we gather
All: **to be with the One**
        who teaches us the meaning of faithfulness.
One: In remembrance, we worship,
All: **lifting our voices to the One**
        who calls us to love one another.
One: In remembrance, we feast,
All: **breaking the Bread that heals us,**
        drinking from the cup that sustains us.

Prayer Of The Evening

It was the beginning of hope
on that night long ago,
Liberating God,
as you prepared to lead
your people to freedom.
As they readied themselves,
you fed them
with your unblemished grace,
so all sin, pain, and bitterness
could be set down and left behind
when it was time
to follow you.

It was the beginning of salvation
on that night long ago,
Servant Lord,
as you prepared your disciples
for all the things that were to happen.

90

You humbled yourself
by washing their feet,
so they could follow you
in service and love
to a world that would reject you
and hang you on a cross.

We retell these stories once again
on this night of remembrance,
Servant's Spirit.
Here is the Bread
that gives us life;
here is the Cup
that slakes our thirst for justice;
here is the towel
with which we wipe the tears
of the brokenhearted;
here is the basin
that cleanses the stains
of the world.

Prepare us for our journey of discipleship,
God in Community, Holy in One,
as we pray as our servant, Jesus Christ,
teaches us, saying,
Our Father ...

Call To Reconciliation

How is it people will recognize us as followers of Jesus? Simply by how we treat one another. Let us confess how we have not loved as Christ has loved us.

Unison Prayer Of Confession

Too often, Holy One, we forget to love you a little bit, much less with our hearts, minds, strengths, and souls. Too easily, we forget to love our neighbors, building higher and higher walls between us. Too quickly, we forget your call to servanthood, hearing instead the accolades and applause of the world.

Forgive us, God of Freedom and Hope. Bring us to the Table of grace, where we will be healed; fill us with your steadfast love; lift us to our feet so we might follow Jesus Christ, our Lord and Savior, into that ministry of servanthood and sacrifice that is our calling.

Silence is kept

Assurance Of Pardon

One: Here is what we have heard: Christ came to teach, to serve, to lead us into the kingdom of God.

**All: We will serve, so others might be set free;
we will teach, so others will know the word of hope;
we will love, so others will know us as Christ's people;
we will do as our servant has done.
Thanks be to God. Amen.**

Good Friday

Isaiah 52:13—53:12
Hebrews 10:16-25 or Hebrews 4:14-16; 5:7-9
John 18:1—19:42

Call To Worship
One: Here, in the midst of these people,
          we come to worship you.
All: **We come with the groans of our lives,**
          and the whispers of hope in our hearts.
One: Here, in the midst of these people,
          we come to remember you.
All: **We come, trusting you have not forgotten us,**
          and that here, promises will be fulfilled.
One: Here, in the midst of these people,
          we come to have our hearts touched.
All: **We come, knowing you hear our souls;**
          we come, to praise you for your steadfast love.

Prayer Of The Day
On this day, God of all Tears,
you call us in the midst
of our busy lives
to look at the suffering and death
of the One who came to carry
the pain of the world into your heart.
Give us eyes to see your love this day.

On this day
you would gather everyone to your side,
Grace of Calvary,
but we leave you to carry the cross alone.
You came simply as love incarnate,
but hate and bitterness
were the gifts we offered to you.

You poured out your love
so our emptiness might be filled.
Give us ears to hear your pain this day.

On this day,
you would pray for us,
Sorrow's Comfort,
for we cannot find the words on our own.
Hear the cries of those in need.
Listen to the sobs of the lonely.
Cradle the whispered hopes of children.
Set free the dreams of prisoners and captives.
Give us hearts to pray with you this day.

God in Community, Holy in One,
we lift our prayers to you in the name of the One
who suffered and died for us this day
and who teaches us to pray, saying,
Our Father ...

Call To Reconciliation

Confident of the hope received by the death of Christ, we can bring our hearts — broken, stained with sin, filled with failings — to the One who sprinkles them with grace, cleansing them with the waters of life.

Unison Prayer Of Confession

Like little children who can wander off in a crowded store, we have lost our way, God of this grim day. We betray you when we do not befriend the poor; we deny you when we are afraid to speak up for the voiceless; we turn our backs on you when we do not do good for others; we crucify you when we harm our family and friends.

At the foot of the cross, we stand with all who have forgotten you and forsaken the way that you offer to us. Forgive us, Lamb of God, and fill us with the mercy, the hope, and the grace you poured out for us, as you gave your life for the sins of the world.

Silence is kept

Assurance Of Pardon

One: Christ has lifted our suffering onto his shoulders, carrying all our hurts and rejections into God's heart. There, God casts them away into the sea of forgetfulness, as we may be restored to hope and lives as new people.

All: Fed with grace, carried in God's arms, we know that we are forgiven. Thanks be to God. Amen.

The Resurrection Of Our Lord
Easter Day

Acts 10:34-43 or Jeremiah 31:1-6
Colossians 3:1-4 or Acts 10:34-43
John 20:1-18 or Matthew 28:1-10

Call To Worship
One: This is the day
All: **when healing touches the suffering,**
when loneliness discovers a family,
when peace caresses the stressed.
One: This is the day the Lord
All: **breaks free of death's clutches,**
rolls away the stone,
folds the grave clothes into a neat pile.
One: This is the day the Lord has made,
All: **the day of sin's defeat,**
the day of resurrection,
the first day of the new creation.
One: This is the day!
All: **Christ is risen! Hallelujah!**

Prayer Of The Day
Surprising God,
early in the morning
before chaos was awake,
you tiptoed quietly past,
and whispered the word
that caused grace and
love to blossom into creation.

Early in the morning
while the disciples slept,
Jesus, Son of the Living God,

you prepared a feast
to fill their emptiness;
you rolled away their hardened hearts
to open them to your grace;
you whispered their names
to awaken them to new life.

Early in the morning
while we are still drowsy,
you sing your songs to us,
Holy Spirit —
hymns of hope, cantatas of compassion,
psalms of peace, litanies of love.

God in Community, Holy in One,
early this morning we bring our prayer to you
as Jesus has taught us, saying,
     Our Father ...

Call To Reconciliation

It was early in the morning when God created all the good and beauty in the universe. It was early in the morning that a baby cried in a manger. It was early in the morning on that first day, when a voice told us that death has been defeated and Jesus is alive in our midst. Let us confess the fear, and the great joy, we bring with us, early in the mornings.

Unison Prayer Of Confession

This morning, Wonderful God, in the company of your church — saints and sinners — we gather to celebrate your life, your ministry, your death and resurrection, and your great love for us. Yet, we know we often leave the celebration here in the sanctuary, as we leave and go back to our homes, our jobs, our fears, our doubts, and our lives.

Bring us a new life, God of the Living, where we are tired and stressed; transform our hardened hearts into fountains of love; forgive us the hurts and harms we have caused; fill us with the joy of your Holy Spirit in the hollows of our souls.

Silence is kept

Assurance Of Pardon

One: God, our Creator, gives us new life;
Christ, our Reconciliation, invites us to a table;
Holy Spirit, our Teacher of the way, the truth, the life;
this is the good news: The tomb is empty,
death is conquered, sin has lost its power.

All: **We are a new people, shaped by the risen Lord into new life forever! Thanks be to God. Amen.**

Easter 2

Acts 2:14a, 22-32
1 Peter 1:3-9
John 20:19-31

Call To Worship

One: Alleluia! Christ is risen!

All: **He is risen indeed! Alleluia!**

One: We have not seen the risen Christ,

All: **but we see him in the lives
of those transformed by grace.**

One: We have not seen Jesus face-to-face,

All: **but we have seen him in the faces
of everyone
whose love encourages us.**

One: We have not touched the wounds from the cross,

All: **but we have been called to bring healing
to the scarred of the world.**

Prayer Of The Day

On the evening
of the first day of creation,
Holy God,
you held out your hands,
full of the grace
we would ever need;
you began to surround us
with all that is good and pleasant.

On the evening
of the first day of Easter,
Defeater of Death,
you walked through the closed doors
of our doubts and fears;

you held us tight
until the warmth of your grace
softened our hardened hearts;
you handed us the gift of peace
to calm our frightened faith.

On the evening
of the first day of following you,
Breath of Peace,
you open our eyes
to the bright color of hope;
you teach us
the glad songs of grace;
you share the most valuable gift of all:
faith.

God in Community, Holy in One,
we lift our prayers to you
as Jesus has taught us, saying,
Our Father ...

Call To Reconciliation

While it is true that we did not put Jesus to death, we are quite aware of all the ways in which we have not followed the paths of life that have been offered to us by God. Let us confess our sins, as we pray, saying,

Unison Prayer Of Confession

We lock the doors of compassion, God of Easter, so that we may share it only with those we believe are deserving. We harden our hearts to the cries around us, because we cannot be completely sure of who is in need. We close our eyes to the suffering around us, believing it will all go away, if we don't look.

Forgive us, Hope of the Ages. You fill us with all the grace we need, not because we are so special, but because we are servants, called to hold out our hands to all in need, even as Jesus Christ, our Lord and Savior, holds out his hands to us, to lead us into your kingdom.

Silence is kept

Assurance Of Pardon

One: From the shadows of life, God brings us into the Light of Christ. From the prison of sin and death, God sets us free to live in hope.

All: The God and Father of our Lord Jesus Christ has raised him from the dead, and given us new life. Thanks be to God. Amen.

Easter 3

Acts 2:14a, 36-41
1 Peter 1:17-23
Luke 24:13-35

Call To Worship

One: Where shattered hearts are made whole,
where wounded souls are healed,
where life is stronger than death;

All: there, the stone has been rolled away.

One: Where the lonely become our friends,
where a stranger is welcomed home,
where hope is stronger than despair;

All: there, we find Jesus walking.

One: Where closed wallets are opened,
where the anxious find serenity,
where love is stronger than hate;

All: there, Jesus is opening our eyes.

One: The stone has been rolled away.
Jesus is our companion on the journey!
Our eyes are opened to the needs of others!

All: Alleluia! Christ is risen!
Alleluia! Christ is with us!

Prayer Of The Day

Splattering the black-blue night
with the twinkling stars
and spinning fluffy clouds
out of the fabric of your hope,
you raised creation out of chaos,
Gracious God,
giving life and calling it good.

Walking with disciples
down grief's lonely road,

you sang of how
God had raised you from the dead,
so that listening, they might believe;
believing, they might understand;
understanding, they might obey;
going forth to invite all
to follow you,
Bread of Life,
to feast on your love forever.

Reaching out your love to us,
so we would touch others;
filling us with your gifts,
so we could be a blessing to the world;
piercing our darkness with hope,
so we might bring healing
to the broken;
you raise us to new life,
Spirit of God.

God in Community, Holy in One,
hear us as we pray, saying,
    Our Father ...

Call To Reconciliation

Here! Christ is here! In our hearts, in our lives, and in our midst.
As on that road to Emmaus, Jesus is with us — teaching, loving,
leading, feeding. Let us confess how we have overlooked the presence of the risen Christ, and ignored the words he whispers to our
hearts, as we pray, saying,

Unison Prayer Of Confession

**We become comfortable, Joyous God, with our lives, with
our faith, with our friends and family. We are so comfortable
that your gospel jars us with your hopes for us. We know we
should tell your story, but doesn't everyone who matters know
it already? We could invite others to your table, but then we**

might have to share. We could welcome the strangers, but worry that they might feel uneasy among so many unfamiliar faces.

Forgive us, God of Easter. Walk with us, so we can become companions to the lost. Welcome us, so we can include the hopeless and homeless. Love us, so we can share that love with everyone we meet on our journey, as we follow Jesus Christ, our Lord and Savior, into life with you.

Silence is kept

Assurance Of Pardon

One: God loves us so much, God will listen to our cries, our prayers, our hopes, and our dreams. God's promises are for all, those who are right beside us, as well as those who live on the other side of the world.

All: **What can we give to God for such grace? We will lift our hearts to God, giving thanks for the mercy that has been given to us. Thanks be to God! Amen.**

Easter 4

Acts 2:42-47
1 Peter 2:19-25
John 10:1-10

Call To Worship

One: This is God's church:
the gate to discernment.

**All: Here, we devote ourselves to God's Word
so we might share the good news.**

One: This is God's house:
the gate to healing.

**All: Here, we taste the bread of life
so we might be made whole.**

One: This is God's community:
the fate to overflowing life.

**All: Here, we are gifted abundantly
so we might be a blessing to God's children.**

Prayer Of The Day

God of Stillness,
your grace murmurs
in our hearts
like a gentle stream;
your goodness and mercy
are the shadows that tag along with us
as we wander the sun-dappled pastures
of creation.

Jesus Christ,
Keeper of our Hearts,
Shepherd of our Souls,
you would lead us down
those paths we find so uncomfortable —

where peace is a way of life,
where enemies are welcomed as family,
where serving others is our calling,
and we would follow you. .

Spirit of Holiness,
Compassion in the Darkest Valley
and Mender of Broken Souls,
our hearts overflow
with the abundance of joy
we find in your kingdom.

God in Community, Holy in One,
hear us as we pray as you have taught us, saying,
Our Father ...

Call To Reconciliation

Christ came to give us life — abundant life. But individually, and as a community, we know how we have wasted our inheritance. Please join me as we confess our sins, so life might be restored to us.

Unison Prayer Of Confession

Why do we live the way we do, Awesome God? Offered green pastures of gentleness and beauty, we choose the sin-littered alleyways of our world. Invited to skip down the paths of hope and healing, we wander off into the ditches of lust and greed. Called to live in community with those who love us and accept us, we close the door in the faces of goodness and mercy, preferring our bitter loneliness.

Forgive us, God of Mercy. Anoint us with the healing touch of your Spirit; call us to your table of grace; strengthen us to follow the shepherd and guardian of our souls, Jesus Christ, our Lord and Savior.

Silence is kept

Assurance Of Pardon

One: Listen! Can you hear them; can you feel them? The still waters of God's mercy and love flow deep within us, cleansing and give us new life.

All: Alleluia! We are forgiven! Thanks be to God. Amen.

Easter 5

Acts 7:55-60
1 Peter 2:2-10
John 14:1-14

Call To Worship

One: We are God's household,
crafted by the architect of creation,

**All: our hearts are shelters for the outcast;
our hands open to the stranger.**

One: We are God's people,
created in the divine image,

**All: to tell others of God's love;
to offer mercy as freely as we have received it.**

One: We are God's children,
called to give of ourselves,

**All: chosen to serve the lost and lonely;
gifted to minister to a hurting world.**

Prayer Of The Day

In a world of war,
we celebrate your peace;
in the midst of oppression,
we welcome that you lead us to freedom;
in the tangled doubts of our hearts,
we celebrate the seed of faith;
in the flood of our tears,
we celebrate the safe ground of hope;
in the pain of hurt and hatred,
we celebrate the family you have given us
that loves us;
in our struggles with sin,
we celebrate our salvation in Christ;

in the face of death,
we celebrate life given to us in the risen Lord.
In every moment, God of all people,
we celebrate all the graces of your heart.
In Jesus' name we pray, even as he has taught us,
Our Father ...

Call To Reconciliation

Considered too rough for their smooth plans, the builders cast out the stone they needed. But God builds salvation on the One who is the foundation of all hopes. Let us confess our sins to God and to one another, trusting we will not be put to shame.

Responsive Prayer Of Confession

One: Lord, you said, "Believe in God, believe also in me."

All: Forgive our unbelief.

One: Lord, you said, "I will come again, and take you to myself, that you may be with me."

All: Forgive our doubts about your future.

One: Lord, you said, "I am the way, the truth, and the life."

**All: Forgive our wandering from your path;
our clutching of the lies of the world;
our desire for more than we need.**

One: Lord, you said, "Have I been with you all this time, and you still do not know me?"

All: Forgive our reluctance to recognize you in others.

One: Lord, you said, "If in my name, you ask me for anything, I will do it."

**All: Forgive us, Precious Savior,
forgive us and grant us your mercy.**

Silence is kept

Assurance Of Pardon

One: You are no longer alone — you are God's Beloved. You are not of this world, but residents of God's kingdom. You, who once had no hope, have been filled with forgiveness.

All: Each one of us, all of us, have received God's mercy in Christ. Forgiven, redeemed, made whole — we are a people made one in faith. Thanks be to God. Amen.

Easter 6

Acts 17:22-31
1 Peter 3:13-22
John 14:15-21

Call To Worship

One: We have come to seek God
**All: who is not as far from us
as we might imagine.**
One: We have come to meet God
**All: who knows us better
than even we can imagine.**
One: We have come to worship God
**All: who has done more for us
than we could dare imagine.**

Prayer Of The Day

Steadfast Love,
you live and breathe life into us;
life that can gentle
the cries of a baby
and the fears of a teenager;
life that can revere creation
and honor a grandparent;
life that can bring hope to the lost,
and healing to those who suffer.

Because you are the Christ,
Child of God,
we know who we are:
those who can be friends
to the rejected of the world;
those who can be joy
to all who have endured loss;

111

those who can be companions
to those whose feet have slipped off the way.

Gift of Grace,
you move gently in us:
so our weakness
may give strength;
so our stuttering words
may bear witness to your love;
so our feeble songs of praise
might echo in the hallways of heaven.

God in Community, Holy in One,
live, and move, and be in us,
even as we pray as we have been taught,

Our Father ...

Call To Reconciliation

God invites us to pray, to lift our words, and even our silence. Let us confess our sins to the One who does not reject our prayers, but welcomes them.

Unison Prayer Of Confession

How often we act as if we do not know you, God of All People! We claim to love Jesus, but we treat those dearest to us as if they were strangers in our house. We orphan neighbors and friends, by not welcoming them into our lives. We are given the Spirit of truth, yet we are filled with deceit and speak lie upon lie.

Even as we speak of how we have not lived as your people, we will account for the hope that is in us: the hope of mercy, the hope of renewal, the hope of faithfulness in following Jesus Christ, who brings us to you, Blessing God.

Silence is kept

Assurance Of Pardon

One: God's constant love has not been taken from us, but is poured out, grace upon grace, into our lives.

All: **Because Christ lives, we will live;**
because Christ serves, we will serve;
because Christ loves, we will love.
Thanks be to God, we are forgiven. Amen.

The Ascension Of Our Lord

Acts 1:1-11
Ephesians 1:15-23
Luke 24:44-53

Call To Worship

One: We gather in this holy place,
        some empty, some filled,
        some whole, some broken,

All: **yearning for the Holy Spirit to fill us.**

One: We come, with these ordinary people,
        who have shown us the way,

All: **trusting that God will continue
        to illumine our hearts.**

One: We surround the table of grace,
        so we might be fed by the Bread of Life,

All: **that graced, we may serve others;
        that healed, we may bring hope to the world.**

Prayer Of The Day

Exalted God,
you are the constant lover
who never forsakes us;
you are the mother
who cradles her children;
you are the teacher
patiently repeating your words for us.
We worship you.

Jesus Christ,
in you we are convinced
God loves us;
through you,
we are formed
into your people;

114

with you,
we serve those
the world ignores.
We follow you.

Holy Spirit,
you are the power
that gives us peace;
you are the wisdom
that reveals the broken
in our midst;
you are the spokesperson
of the voiceless
to whom we are deaf.
We welcome you.

God in Community, Holy in One,
we lift our prayers to you
as Jesus taught us, saying,
   Our Father ...

Call To Reconciliation

Called to proclaim repentance, we are reluctant to look at our own failings. Invited to witness to God's loving forgiveness of sins, we would rather not speak aloud of our own. Let us trust in the One who offers us hope and healing, as we pray together, saying,

Unison Prayer Of Confession

You call us to proclaim a gospel we find difficult to practice, God Most High. We watch our clocks to make sure we spend more time with ourselves than with you. We are hesitant to witness to your power from on high, as we are uncertain of your presence in our lives.

Forgive us, God of Light. Fill us with the healing presence of your Spirit, that we may proclaim your good news, as we participate in the life and suffering of our world, as did your Son, our Lord and Savior, Jesus Christ.

Silence is kept

Assurance Of Pardon

One: Choosing to set aside judgment, God gives us justice;
        choosing to let go of punishment, God fills us with peace;
        choosing to release anger, God's steadfast love rests upon
        us.

All: **Forgiven, redeemed, restored — we will tell everyone,
        through the lives we lead, what God has done for us.
        Thanks be to God. Amen.**

Easter 7

Acts 1:6-14
1 Peter 4:12-14; 5:6-11
John 17:1-11

Call To Worship
One: The hour has come to worship our God,
All: **to gather as people of faith**
        to glorify the God of all grace.
One: The time has come to devote ourselves to prayer,
All: **to bring the burdens we carry,**
        to lift our hopes to the God who hears us.
One: The hour has come to rejoice and make God's name known,
All: **to lift a song of thanksgiving,**
        to praise God for all our blessings.

Prayer Of The Day
Your love is so limitless
that the needy receive goodness,
and the prisoner finds
a well-paying job;
the homeless find your heart
open to them,
and all can place their worries
in your hands.
Parent of Orphans,
we will make your name known
to all the world.

We gaze at the sky
looking for you,
when you can be found
in the laughing play of children;

117

we wonder
where you have gone,
while you are all around us
in our sisters and brothers.
Cloud Rider,
we will sing of your name
to all the world.

When our hearts
are hardened by fears,
you melt them
with your hope;
when our lips
can only utter boasts,
you teach us
songs of humility.
Caregiver of Widows,
we will exult your name
in all the world.

We will make your name known,
God in Community, Holy in One, — Amen
even as we pray as we have been taught,
    Our Father ...

Call To Reconciliation

    When we look to God in prayer, are we looking for condemnation and punishment? Or, do we look for the One who promises to forgive us and make us new? Let us pray to God for mercy, as we offer our confessions, saying,

Unison Prayer Of Confession

    We cannot put it off any longer, Gracious God, it is time to confess our unfaithfulness. Our appetites for all things threaten to devour us like hungry animals. We are reluctant to humble ourselves to serve others, believing we are special. We are afraid to share in the sufferings of children and the elderly.

118

Forgive us, Voice of Mercy and Hope. Bless us with grace and life, so we might rejoice in your love, tell of your faithfulness, and join Jesus Christ, our Lord and Savior, in making you known to all people.

Silence is kept

Assurance Of Pardon

One: Unfailing love, the Spirit of healing, the life of faith in Christ — all are Easter gifts God offers to us.

All: **We rejoice and are glad. We are blessed: with mercy, with hope, with joy. Thanks be to God. Amen.**

The Day Of Pentecost

Acts 2:1-21
1 Corinthians 12:3b-13
John 7:37-39

Call To Worship

One: The day of Pentecost is upon us.

**All: Those who have been touched by tongues of fire
can speak as though in native languages.**

One: In worship together, let us share with each other.

All: Let us share our bread, our wine, and our prayers.

One: We come to the Lord's table.

All: It is spread before us.

Prayer Of The Day

One: Spirit of the Living God,
visit us again on this day of Pentecost,

All: come, Holy Spirit.

One: Like a rushing wind that sweeps away all barriers,

All: come, Holy Spirit.

One: Like tongues of fire that set our hearts aflame,

All: come, Holy Spirit.

One: With speech that unites the confusion of our languages,

All: come, Holy Spirit.

One: With love that overlaps the boundaries of race and nation,

All: come, Holy Spirit.

One: With power from above to make our weakness strong,

**All: come, Holy Spirit, come as we pray, saying,
Our Father ...**

Call To Reconciliation

We admit that in our lives we forget to cooperate with each other, with the Holy Spirit, with Jesus, and with the Father. We forget to think of God and of God's grace. Please join me as we confess our lives to the listening God.

Unison Prayer Of Confession

We ask your grace in our lives for our many sins: for ignoring people who are in need, for disrespecting our loved ones, and for speaking harsh words rather than sympathetic ones to those who do not understand. We continually judge people by their actions instead of as children of God. We fail to do unto others in our communities and in our world as we would have them do unto us.

Forgive us now, for we repent, O God.

Silence is kept

Assurance Of Pardon

One: All the promises of God find their "yes" in Christ. That is why we utter the "Amen" through him, to the glory of God. It is God who has put his seal upon us and given us the Spirit in our hearts as a guarantee.

All: **In Christ, by the power of the Spirit, we are redeemed. Praise God, from whom all blessings flow!**

The Holy Trinity

Genesis 1:1—2:4a
2 Corinthians 13:11-13
Matthew 28:16-20

Call To Worship
One: God, who created all things and named them "good,"
has shaped us in the divine image.
All: **We come, with grace-filled hearts,**
into the presence of our Creator.
One: Jesus, who led the way by carrying a cross,
has brought us into the kingdom of God.
All: **We come, our brokenness made whole,**
into the presence of our Redeemer.
One: The Holy Spirit, who brings us together from many places,
calls us to be the household of God.
All: **We come, all walls broken down,**
into the presence of our Sustainer.

Prayer Of The Day
Imaginative God,
you spoke,
and your Word
carved towering peaks
and cascading streams;
your breath stirred chaos,
and stars glimmer in the long night,
the sun trumpets new life —
you are Creation's Architect!

Jesus Christ,
the poor and needy praise you,
for you are their brother;
little children climb into your lap,
for you are their safety;

sinners whisper your name,
for you are our hope —
you are the Word made Flesh!

Spirit of Holiness,
you are the bracing wind
that drives away our sins;
you are the fire that cleanses us
by dancing in our hearts;
you are the morning dew
that moistens our desert lips —
you are the Breath of God!

God in Community, Holy in One,
we lift our prayers to you as we have been taught, saying,
Our Father ...

Call To Reconciliation

Do people see God when they look at us? Do they hear Jesus' words of welcome and hope when we speak? Do they see the fresh Spirit acting in our lives? In these moments, we must be honest with God as to how we have not lived up to our calling to be God's people. Let us pray together, saying,

Unison Prayer Of Confession

God of glory, grace, and wisdom, you have made us in your image, but we do not always show your gracious face. We are called to follow the Christ, but fatigued by the stresses of our lives, we often do not have the energy or enthusiasm. When we see the Spirit standing with the oppressed and outcast, we, too, often turn and walk the other way.
Creator God,
Master of the Universe,
have mercy on us;
Jesus Christ,
Brother and Sister to the Poor,

have mercy on us;
Holy Spirit,
Comfort of the Brokenhearted,
have mercy on us.

Silence is kept

Assurance Of Pardon
One: Here is the good news: God continues to create out of the chaos and brokenness of our lives, filling our hearts with love, transforming our despair into hope, and shaping our selfishness into servanthood.

All: **What marvelous news! God loves us, Christ redeems us, and the Spirit calls us to service. Thanks be to God. Amen.**

Charge And Benediction
One: God, who created you in the divine image, sends you forth;

All: **we go, to reflect the presence of our Creator to everyone we meet.**

One: Jesus, who has redeemed you, has established God's kingdom in our midst;

All: **we go, to bring healing to the broken of the world.**

One: The Holy Spirit, who calls you to be God's people, goes with you to many places;

All: **we go, to tear down the walls that divide us, and to build lives of hope for all of God's children.**

One: And now, may the peace of the rolling waves,
       the peace of the silent mountains,
       the peace of the singing stars,
       and the deep, deep peace of the Prince of Peace
       be with you now and forever.
       Amen.

Proper 4
Pentecost 2
Ordinary Time 9

Genesis 6:9-22; 7:24; 8:14-19
Romans 1:16-17; 3:22b-28 (29-31)
Matthew 7:21-29

Call To Worship

One: Be still!

**All: The One who cradled the remnant of creation
in the cleansing waters calls us here.**

One: Be still! And know this:

**All: At the present time, God cradles us in safety
even as fear floods all around us.**

One: Be still! And know who God is.

**All: The One who is with us in every moment:
past, present, and future.**

Prayer Of The Day

In every city center
where lives teeter on the edge;
in every suburban home
where lives can be trapped
in the quicksand of complacency:
you are there, Helping God.

In every corridor of power
where nations can hurl insults
or whisper hope;
in every prejudice
rooted in fear,
in every grace-filled conversation
between strangers: you are there,
Strength of the World.

In every heart that welcomes
the broken and beaten-down of the world;
in every reconciling embrace
of those we once boasted were our enemies:
you are there, Spirit of Refuge.

God in Community, Holy in One,
early in the morning,
your glad rivers of hope and joy flow through us,
as we lift our prayers, saying,
  Our Father ...

Call To Reconciliation
When we gather to praise our God, we remember that we are
people who tend to choose our will over God's. Accepting God's
power to create us as new people in Christ, let us confess our sins
before God and one another, as we pray,

Responsive Prayer Of Confession
One: In the lonely neighbor next door, you come to us,
            but we do not recognize you;
        in the cries of children sleeping in the street, you call,
            but we do not hear you;
        in the laughing hug of an old friend, you bless us,
            but we do not feel you.
All: **Forgive us, and make us new.**
One: In the immigrant who sits beside us on the bus,
        you accept us,
            but we cannot shake your hand;
        in the family member who tells us to "forget it,"
        you forgive us,
            but we cannot let go of what they have done to us.
All: **Forgive us, and make us new.**
One: In a broken world, we see your mission,
            but we insist on doing everything our way;
        in the outcast, the poor, the needy, we find you,
            but we do not care what is happening to you;

126

in your death and resurrection, we find life,
but we dare not believe you.

All: **Forgive us, and make us new.**

Silence is kept

Assurance Of Pardon

One: There is no shame in the good news, only hope, only life, only joy, only peace.

All: **Even now, God is forgiving us; even now, God is making us new. Thanks be to God. Amen.**

Proper 5
Pentecost 3
Ordinary Time 10

Genesis 12:1-9
Romans 4:13-25
Matthew 9:9-13, 18-26

Call To Worship

One: The sinners, the saints;
the broken, the whole:
all come together in this sacred space.

**All: We come rejoicing
in the One who gives life.**

One: The doubters, the devout;
the wonderers, the wanderers;
all are called by the same Lord.

**All: We come, some eagerly, some fearfully,
to follow Jesus the Christ.**

One: The hesitant, the heroic,
the grandparents, the little children;
all are embraced in God's love.

**All: We come with whispers of hope
and glad shouts of joy on our lips.**

Prayer Of The Day

Without fail, you find them,
Searching God;
in every generation,
people respond to your gracious call
to journey into the unknown:
old people teetering on retirement,
a man doing a job for which
everyone despises him,

128

a woman speaking truths
that no one wants to hear.
But they hear you,
and in listening,
their lives —
and ours —
are transformed by your promise.
So, in this time,
in this place,
to this generation,
call us.
This we pray in the name of Jesus,
who taught us to say when we pray:
    Our Father ...

Call To Reconciliation

"Is it true?" — that's the question we bring to this place in this time. God's promises, God's love, God's salvation — is it all true: for you, for me, for us? Let us confess our fears and our failings, as we approach the One we believe is truth.

Unison Prayer Of Confession
Jesus, sitting with sinners and tax collectors:
    you watch us jostle for a place
    at the head table.
Jesus, walking along and calling outcasts
into your community:
    you see us hurry past the homeless
    and the lost.
Jesus, healer of those the world looks down
its nose at:
    you weep as we overlook
    the broken in our communities.
Jesus, Dear Desirer of Mercy,
forgive us.

129

Silence is kept

Assurance Of Pardon

One: The promise rests on God's grace, not on our best efforts.
         At any time, in every moment, God's constant love heals
         our hearts, mends our brokenness, and restores us to life.

All: Thanks be to God. Amen.

Proper 6
Pentecost 4
Ordinary Time 11

Genesis 18:1-15 (21:1-7)
Romans 5:1-8
Matthew 9:35—10:8 (9-23)

Call To Worship

One: On an ordinary Sunday,
we come to worship God.

All: We come, trusting God will speak to us;
we come, hoping God will surprise us.

One: On this day, like every other day,
we seek to follow Jesus.

All: We follow, believing Jesus will be with us;
we follow, hoping Jesus will work through us.

One: On this day,
we lift our souls to God's Spirit;

All: we open our hearts, that the Spirit may fill us;
we open our hands that we might be a gift to others.

Prayer Of The Day

The little child struggling with fears,
the grandfather facing failing health,
the parent who lies awake until the early morning hours,
the teenager pressured by peers,
the lonely who are prey to con artists,
all of us with ordinary aches, pains, and worries;
each is cradled in your infinite compassion,
Tender God.

Those who work through the night,
those who walk the street,
those who are called exceptional,

those who are differently gifted,
those who are filled with doubts,
those who spill over in laughter,
the youngest,
the oldest,
the ordinary;
each is called by you,
Lord Jesus.

Joyous praisers of your name,
seekers of hope,
those walled out by prejudice and hate,
babies who cry from hunger,
the poor who share their last coin
with those in greater need;
all the ordinary people around the world
are not disappointed by your presence,
Spirit of Hope.

God in Community, Holy in One,
hear us as we lift our voices,
praying as Jesus has taught us, saying,
Our Father ...

Call To Reconciliation

This is all the proof we need: It was when we were least able to save ourselves that God did it for us in Christ Jesus. Because we trust that God forgives us, let us bring our confessions to God, praying,

Unison Prayer Of Confession

Merciful God, if we committed extraordinary sins, we might feel a need to confess to you. But our failings seem so everyday and petty:
    ignoring our friends and families,
    forgetting to look after creation,
    hoarding the blessing you have given to us,
    following political agendas instead of Jesus.

Forgive us, Compassionate God, for we not only harm others and our world by our sins, but we break your heart. Call us again, and strengthen us to follow in the footsteps of Jesus — sitting with the sufferers, offering ourselves in obedience to you, opening our hearts to all your children. In the name of Jesus, we pray.

Silence is kept

Assurance Of Pardon

One: Christ has died for us — can God's love be made any clearer to us? By this gift, we enter into God's kingdom, and are graced to serve others.

**All: Forgiven, gifted, restored, called;
we are God's people. Amen.**

Proper 7
Pentecost 5
Ordinary Time 12

Genesis 21:8-21
Romans 6:1b-11
Matthew 10:24-39

Call To Worship

One: There is no one like you,
God of Abraham and Sarah.

**All: We ask for signs,
and you fill us with surprises.**

One: There is no one like you,
God of Hagar and Ishmael.

**All: We cry out in our need,
and you listen to our voices.**

One: There is no one like you,
God of each and every person.

**All: We ask for power
and you give us the humility
to serve all your children.**

Prayer Of The Day

God of those cast out
and of the abandoned,
you enter into the chaos of our lives
with the silence of love;
as we choke on bitter memories,
you touch us with healing;
when we wander
the wilderness of our world,
you bring us home to your heart.

Jesus Christ,
Sin's Conqueror,
into our deepest pain
where we can find no hope,
you dare to enter;
when we gasp in fear,
you reach out to hold our hearts;
when we face death,
you stride out of the grave
to lead us to the boulevards
of the kingdom.

Spirit of Gentleness,
you are the mist
shimmering over the valleys,
stirring the waters of creation;
you are the dew
bathing the flowers every morning,
anointing us with resurrection's grace.

God in Community, Holy in One,
we lift our prayer to you, as Jesus has taught us,
   Our Father ...

Call To Reconciliation
Whether we whisper, weep, or shout, we can trust God to hear us and to respond. Even when we fail to follow Jesus — especially when we fail to follow — God does not turn away, but cradles us in the steadfast arms of mercy and grace. Let us confess our sins together, praying,

Unison Prayer Of Confession
We confess to you, God our God, that some of the stories in the Bible trouble us more than the news we hear each day. Some of the words that Jesus speaks make us more uncomfortable than the cries of those in need in our communities. And while our baptism may be a sign of your invisible grace, many of those around us do not find us to be very gracious people.

135

Forgive us, Gracious God. Save us and give us the strength to be willing to take up whatever task you give us, and the faith to be willing to lose our lives for others, so we might find life forever with you, through Jesus Christ, our Lord and Savior.

Silence is kept

Assurance Of Pardon

One: This is the good news: God hears our prayers, our cries, and our confessions. God listens to every longing of our hearts. And, in Christ, we receive new life. We are free, free to walk in the light of the Lord.

All: **This is what we will do. We will open our hearts to God's grace; we will live as people who have died to sin and live for Christ. Thanks be to God. Amen.**

Proper 8
Pentecost 6
Ordinary Time 13

Genesis 22:1-14
Romans 6:12-23
Matthew 10:40-42

Call To Worship

One: With joy and celebration,
God welcomes us to this place.
All: How good it is to gather in God's house!
One: With joy and celebration,
we welcome one another.
**All: We greet each other by name;
we are equal in God's kingdom.**
One: We open our hearts, to welcome God's love;
we open our arms, to welcome God's people.
All: Here, every single one of God's children is welcome.

Prayer Of The Day

You have invited us
to this place,
Accepting God,
for this is where you want us.
Here, we learn to trust you,
and to faithfully follow where you lead us.
Here, we learn to listen to you,
and hear the words of life,
of hope, and of healing.
Here, we learn to bring everything to you —
even our pain, especially our brokenness —
that we might be made whole.

Pilgrim Jesus,
you are with us in this place,
and in every place
where we live, work, play, pray.
If we dare to trust
this good news,
we discover that grace,
which sets us free
to treat one another
as sisters and brothers;
to use that grace
to break down every barrier;
to live that grace
in every moment of our lives.

We would receive you
into our hearts,
Abiding Spirit,
knowing that you have brought us together,
and by the gift of your presence,
we are no longer strangers
but friends and neighbors
in your kingdom.

God in Community, Holy in One,
hear us as we pray as Jesus taught us, saying,
Our Father ...

Call To Reconciliation

Created to live with one another and our God, we know the truth about our shattered lives and relationships. Yet, out of this brokenness, God shapes new people, giving every one of us a new start. Let us confess those things that separate us from one another, that we might be made one in Christ.

Unison Prayer Of Confession

In your house, there is room for all; at your table, we find a place set for us. Yet we admit, Inviting God, that we find it difficult to be as accepting as you and we find it easy to shoulder others away from your feast. You fling wide the doors to your kingdom, Welcoming God, but we are quick to try to shut them to those who are different from us. Your heart is open so that all might experience your grace, and we reluctantly remember our ungracious words and deeds.

Forgive us, God of Every Person: heal our broken lives; mend our fragmented souls. Open our hearts to your vision of the kingdom where all are welcome, all are affirmed, all are beloved — even as we receive these gifts from Jesus Christ, our Lord and Savior.

Silence is kept

Assurance Of Pardon

One: Can it be any clearer? God has created us to be a family — sisters, brothers, neighbors, friends. No longer strangers, we are all welcome in the kingdom of love, grace, and hope.

All: **In Christ, we are one. There are no barriers, no differences, and no divisions. We are a new people, forgiven and made whole. Thanks be to God. Amen.**

Proper 9
Pentecost 7
Ordinary Time 14

Genesis 24:34-38, 42-49, 58-67
Romans 7:15-25a
Matthew 11:16-19, 25-30

Call To Worship

One: Come to our God,
all who hunger for life,

All: **for it is God who nourishes us
at the table of grace.**

One: Come to our God,
all who are worn-out by life,

All: **for it is God who provides
the rest we need.**

One: Come to our God,
all who are weighed down,

All: **for it is our God who carries
our burdens with us.**

Prayer Of The Day

Eternal God,
you sing a song
of silence
to our noisy hearts,
inviting us to still
our fidgeting souls,
and find our peace
in your cupped hands
that cradle us.

Jesus Christ,
Wanderer of the Kingdom,

you are called
to reveal God to us
and do so in
the tenderness of your touch,
the gentleness of your words,
the goodness of your heart, and
the peace of your shared yoke.

Spirit of Rest,
your childlike presence
opens our eyes
to the wonders of the world.
As we hand you
our anger, our hurt, and our sin,
may our burdens
become our songs of joy,
even as we pray as Jesus taught us, saying,
Our Father ...

Call To Reconciliation

Fretful, agitated, longing for more and more of this and that, we spend our lives in a never-ending, never-fulfilled search for that which satisfies. But Christ knows that we will only find the end of our journey in God, and so invites us to that peaceful place known as God's heart. Help us let go of our burdens of anger, hurt, and sin so we can find our rest.

Unison Prayer Of Confession

We are so skilled at being in control, at taking charge, Sabbath-taking God, that we are not very good at resting. We think we have to be constantly busy, so we have no time for you. We are trained to be extremely productive, and so create our harried, stress-filled lives.

Forgive us, Shalom-giving God. Help us to let go of our distractions, so you can act in us; calm our creaturely activity, so you can re-create us; help us to follow Jesus, not only into discipleship, but into our rest with you.

Silence is kept

Assurance Of Pardon

One: It sounds so simple, we think it is too simple. But which is the burden you would choose: hate or love, anger or forgiveness, pain or peace? God invites us to receive the gifts that make it possible to have lives of faithful obedience.

All: This is the good news: God forgives us and takes our burdens from us. We would let go of them and welcome hope, joy, and grace into our lives. Thanks be to God. Amen.

Proper 10
Pentecost 8
Ordinary Time 15

Genesis 25:19-34
Romans 8:1-11
Matthew 13:1-9, 18-23

Call To Worship

One: On this midsummer's day,
      we gather as God's people

**All: to hear stories of folks just like us —
      who make mistakes, choose favorites, and judge others.**

One: On this midsummer's day,
      we struggle as God's people

**All: easily distracted by a culture with too many choices,
      our lives don't even have room for God.**

One: On this midsummer's day,
      we worship as God's people

**All: trying to listen so we will be transformed,
      keeping our eyes open to see the way God offers.**

Prayer Of The Day

Deep in the rich soul of our hearts,
you sow the seeds of grace,
God of the Harvest.
And there, the seeds take root,
blossoming and flourishing:
light to offer those in the shadows,
the practices to hone our faith,
the hope that springs up in unexpected moments,
the prayers and support of strangers.
Goodness and mercy
are the living waters that nurture

143

this tender growth within us,
and your Son's Light
brings forth the fruit
you imagined to be in us:
love, joy, peace, patience,
kindness, generosity, faithfulness,
gentleness, self-control.
Continue to plant, to nurture,
to water, and to tend your most precious crop,
those who seek to faithfully follow Jesus
even as we pray as he teaches us,
   Our Father ...

Call To Reconciliation

Nothing, nothing, not one thing can separate us from God! Death cannot do it, nor the foolish lives we lead. Sin cannot keep us apart from God, nor can the pain we cause others. With that promise — and with that freedom — let us confess our lives to God, saying,

Unison Prayer Of Confession

We used to think that the people in the Bible were giants of the faith, God of Lives, but then we discover how much they are like us, and we them. Like Isaac and Rebekah, we choose favorites, causing pain to those who most need our love and attention. Like Esau, we quickly let go of the promises given to us, so we can gratify our desires instantly. Like Jacob, we struggle with your claim on our lives, always in conflict with your hopes for us.

Forgive us, Loving God. Because we are so much like the people in the Bible, we are heirs of your promises, recipients of your grace, and sharers of your mercy. Your Son, our Lord and Savior, Jesus Christ, sows the seeds of discipleship in our hearts. May we not choke them off, but let them grow each and every day of our lives.

Silence is kept

Assurance Of Pardon

One: This is good news: In Christ there is no judgment. We are filled with grace, with hope, and with joy.

All: Thanks be to God, who gives us new life. Amen.

Proper 11
Pentecost 9
Ordinary Time 16

Genesis 28:10-19a
Romans 8:12-25
Matthew 13:24-30, 36-43

Call To Worship

One: We come to the One
        who knows all the facts about our lives;

All: **we are open books to God,
        who writes on every page.**

One: We approach the One
        who knows what we are thinking;

All: **our thoughts, our fears, our hopes
        are all known by God.**

One: We worship the One
        who is always with us,
        in front of us, behind us, around us;

All: **what a wonderful God!
        How blessed we are!**

Prayer Of The Day

You we praise, Searching God,
for your presence surrounds us in every moment;
you reside in our hearts.
There is no cobwebbed corner
that is not claimed by your love.
The gate of heaven
is open to us in our moments of doubt,
as well as our moments of faith.
In our times of rest,

you whisper hope to us;
you awaken us, inviting us
to work in your kingdom.
Caller of our Hearts,
may we listen to your voice
and serve you with grace,
even as we pray as we have been taught, saying,
    Our Father ...

Call To Reconciliation

When we fail to live as God's people, we naturally look for places to hide. But God seeks us out, not to condemn or punish, but to comfort, to forgive, and to bring us home. Let us stop playing hide-and-seek, with God, as we confess our sins together, saying,

Unison Prayer Of Confession
I've tried to hide from your searching gaze,
Love's Delight,
I've climbed mountains,
I've gone deep within caverns,
I've flown to the farthest edges of my soul.
And wherever I go —
you are waiting for me!
Even in the darkest recesses of my heart,
your light shines on me.
Lost —
I am found;
afraid to speak of my sinfulness —
you hear my stumbling words before I shape them;
unable to help myself —
you redeem me through the love and grace
of Jesus Christ, my Lord and Savior.

Silence is kept

Assurance Of Pardon

One: In our deepest sorrow, God comforts us;
in our darkest moments, God forgives us;
in our greatest joy, God is with us.

All: **The One who knows us at our worst, loves us best. We trust that God will hold us close, this day and forever. Thanks be to God, we are forgiven! Amen.**

Proper 12
Pentecost 10
Ordinary Time 17

Genesis 29:15-28
Romans 8:26-39
Matthew 13:31-33, 44-52

Call To Worship

One: We come, to proclaim God's majesty,
        giving thanks to the One who has called us
        to speak to the world.

All: **We will sing praises to God,**
        telling of all the wonders of our lives.

One: We come, thankful that we are God's children,
        rejoicing as we worship our God.

All: **We know that God is always with us;**
        that the word gives us life and hope.

One: We come, because God keeps promises;
        God's faithfulness is everlasting.

All: **Praise God! Praise God!**

Prayer Of The Day

Searcher of Hearts,
you have brought us to this place,
not to scold us or condemn us,
but to embrace us with your forgiveness;
to comfort us with your hope.

Heart of God,
you cast out your net
so that all might be brought
into your kingdom;
your grace is hidden deep within us,
that it might be revealed in our lives.

149

Companion Spirit,
when we cannot pray,
you whisper from our hearts,
lifting us to the One from whom nothing can separate us.

God in Community, Holy in One,
hear us as we pray as we have been taught, saying,
Our Father ...

Call To Reconciliation

It is not our past that keeps us from God, for that is behind us. It is not our present, for God is with us in these days. And our future moments are held in God's hands. What the apostle Paul says is true: nothing can separate us from God. And whatever sins we have committed, God's forgiveness and love take them away forever. Join me, as we pray together, saying,

Unison Prayer Of Confession

What then are we to say about our sins, Loving God? We know that we worship power, rather than serving in humility. We worry about things over which we have no control, instead of trusting in you. We fear death, when you have promised we will live with you forever.

Forgive us, Grace of the World, for thinking that our sins are more powerful than your mercy. Because of the love of Christ Jesus, our Lord, proven on the cross and fulfilled in the resurrection, we are new people, forgiven and made whole.

Silence is kept

Assurance Of Pardon

One: Who has earned the right to judge us? Only Christ. Christ died for us, Christ has risen for us, Christ reigns in power over us; Christ even prays for us!

All: **This is the love that binds us to God forever. There is nothing in this world, or the next, that will keep us from being God's children. Thanks be to God. Amen.**

150

Proper 13
Pentecost 11
Ordinary Time 18

Genesis 32:22-31
Romans 9:1-5
Matthew 14:13-21

Call To Worship

One: We come to this place of worship,
to encounter the One who has called us here.

**All: This Holy One — our God —
is with us in every moment.**

One: God is in our celebrations and joys,
God is in our darkest nights of loneliness.

**All: This Holy God — our God —
blesses us and calls us by name.**

One: As night fades before the coming light,
we meet the One who saves us —
even from ourselves.

**All: This God — our Holy God —
touches us with the spirit of hope.**

Prayer Of The Day

In the darkest moments
of our lives,
Intriguing God,
we have struggled with you,
believing that if we were to beat you,
you would have to give us whatever we want,
not realizing you have already blessed us
with everything we need in life.

151

When our hunger for hope
overwhelms us,
Gentle Jesus,
you fill us with your presence;
when our need for more and more
would pull us further and further
away from you,
you heal us of our desires;
when we look away from those in need,
your tears of compassion
cleanse our hearts.

We would leave our pain behind us,
and run through your streams
of living waters,
Spirit of God,
that we might embrace
our sisters and brothers in peace,
knowing that our broken relationships
have been made whole.

God in Community, Holy in One,
we lift our prayers to you,
in the name of Jesus Christ, our Lord and Savior,
    Our Father ...

Call To Reconciliation

We pick on sisters and brothers, we argue with our spouses,
we fight with friends and neighbors — we all live broken lives. We
even end up struggling with God, seeking to make God do our
bidding. But it is God who can heal our brokenness, God who can
reconcile our differences, God who can make us families once again.
Let us confess our sins together, seeking God's promised blessing
for each of us.

Unison Prayer Of Confession

Here at the river's edge, Healing God, we are hesitant to cross over. For on the other side are all the people we have hurt. On that far shore is everyone we have ridiculed, scorned, and ignored. Across the water stand the poor, the homeless, and the lost — all those we have looked down on, believing that they are beneath us. On the other bank stands the cross we must carry if we are to follow Jesus.

Before we can cross, Most Holy One, we must struggle with you. We cannot meet the others, if we have not encountered you. Forgive us and reconcile us, not only to them, but to yourself. Bless us, so we would be a blessing to them. Rename us and carry us across the river as faithful disciples of the One we are blessed to call our Lord and Savior, Jesus Christ.

Silence is kept

Assurance Of Pardon

One: Here, face-to-face, God meets us. Here, face-to-face, we can speak every longing in our hearts. Here, face-to-face, God forgives us.

All: **Here, face-to-face, we meet the One who has great compassion for us, and who forgives us of every sin. Thanks be to God. Amen.**

Proper 14
Pentecost 12
Ordinary Time 19

Genesis 37:1-4, 12-28
Romans 10:5-15
Matthew 14:22-33

Call To Worship

One: Scripture tells us of how Jesus once invited Peter
       to step out in faith onto the deep waters.

**All: We are also invited to step out of our safety,
       our security, and walk toward Jesus.**

One: Peter became afraid and,
       in his fear, began to sink.

**All: Like Peter, we are afraid and cry out,
       "Lord, save us."**

One: The One who has power over all creation
       comes to save us.

**All: We will be saved by the One
       who is God's Son!**

Prayer Of The Day

All around us are signs of your presence,
God-in-Christ.
Where the oppressed receive justice,
you will be found;
where the hungry are being fed,
you are on the serving line;
when the blind receive their sight,
you show them the glories of creation;
where the stranger is welcomed,
you are holding out your arms;

when the prisoners are set free,
you step forward in hope with them;
where promises are broken,
you reach out to mend shattered hearts.

And you are not alone,
for you call us to work beside you
in every place where you are,
with every person you serve,
with every breath you give us,
with every gift with which we have been blessed.
Help us to love you and one another more
than any award, job, or recognition,
even as we pray as Jesus has taught us, saying,
   Our Father ...

Call To Reconciliation

   God alone deserves our loyalty and trust, but often our faith
sinks and our trust is blown away by the storms of life. Let us tell
God of our sins, that we might know forgiveness, and live forever
with our God. Join me as we pray, saying,

Unison Prayer Of Confession

   **Too often, Waiting God, we have so little faith that we be-
gin to sink, and we trust the world to save us. We find it so easy
to drown in the temptations of the world. Our boats seem so
sturdy and safe that we hesitate to step out of them into new
ways of life.**

   **Save us, Holy God, save us! Reach out your hand to those
dying in fear and drowning in doubt. Reach out your hand, as
Jesus did to Peter, not because we deserve rescue, but because
you love us enough to save us, from ourselves, from sin, and
from death. This we pray, in Jesus' name.**

Silence is kept

Assurance Of Pardon

One: We cannot avoid the truth that we are sinners. But the greater truth is that we are forgiven sinners. Through God's love in Christ Jesus, we set aside all that is past, and step out, in courage and faith, into God's future for us.

All: **We trust God's promises, we trust Christ's resurrection, we trust the Spirit who works in and through us. Thanks be to God. Amen.**

Proper 15
Pentecost 13
Ordinary Time 20

Genesis 45:1-15
Romans 11:1-2a, 29-32
Matthew 15:(10-20) 21-28

Call To Worship
One: How good it is to gather as God's people!
All: **Here, there are no barriers between us;**
        here, we make no distinctions among people.
One: When we come together as God's family,
All: **it is as if the sacred water of baptism**
        is once more running down our cheeks.
One: When we rejoice together,
        when we pray together,
        when we serve together,
All: **we know the abundant life**
        God has promised us.

Prayer Of The Day
Welcoming God,
your covenant with your people
is never broken;
your call to us is never taken back;
your invitation to all
to be a part of your family
is never revoked.

Accepting Christ,
there is not any place
you will not go
to bring God's grace to others.

In you,
the enemy is made a friend;
the broken are made whole;
the orphan finds a family.

Embracing Spirit,
your gentleness falls upon us,
and our fears of rejection vanish;
your truth is whispered in our ears,
and our arms open to strangers;
your peace is poured into our souls,
and we are reconciled to those we have hurt;
your love opens our shuttered hearts,
and we recognize our brothers and sisters
around us.

God in Community, Holy in One,
in you we receive life forevermore.
Hear us as we pray as Jesus has taught us:
Our Father ...

Call To Reconciliation

Even as we gather to praise God, we must remember that too often we prefer our way to God's. Because God can make us new people, we dare to speak to God of all that we have done this past week that did not reflect the holy within us.

Unison Prayer Of Confession

Given the chance, God of this day, we know we will choose to follow the world and not you. We show this by how we treat our families and friends. We reveal our choices in our desire for more and more of everything. We expose our lack of faith by our trust in the temptations of our culture, rather than in your call to obedience and service.

We come to you, Helper of the Weak, looking for mercy. You do not give us the crumbs of your heart, but the fullness of grace. You do not turn your back on us, but run toward us to sweep us into your loving arms. You come into our broken world

that we might be carried into your kingdom of hope and joy. You give us new life, life forever, through Jesus Christ, our Lord and Savior.

Silence is kept

Assurance Of Pardon

One: It is God who hears you, God who forgives you, God who loves you, and God who gives you new life.

All: **Even now, God is with us, filling our hearts with peace and joy. Thanks be to God. Amen.**

Proper 16
Pentecost 14
Ordinary Time 21

Exodus 1:8—2:10
Romans 12:1-8
Matthew 16:13-20

Call To Worship
One: In a time of bitterness and pain,
All: **God raised up Moses,**
        and changed the lives of a people.
One: From the shadow of death,
All: **God raised up Jesus,**
        and changed the lives of all people.
One: In every time, and in every place,
All: **God raises up witnesses,**
        people whose lives are changed forever.

Prayer Of The Day
Like Miriam with Moses,
you watch over us,
Ever-seeing God.
You do not leave us
to drift on the currents
of the world;
you will not give us over
to the power of evil;
you have not left us alone,
but gifted us with your body,
the church.

Christ of Compassion,
you could have used the wise,
but you work through the foolish.

You could have chosen
the most gifted talkers,
but you speak through children.
You could command us
to do anything you wish,
but you beg us
to open our lives
to God's Wisdom.

Helper Spirit,
when we are reluctant
to part with our treasures,
you fill us with generosity.
When we are hesitant
to help others,
you make us passionate to serve.
When we are loud and afraid,
you surround us
with loving sisters and brothers.

God in Community, Holy in One,
hear us as we pray as we have been taught,
    Our Father ...

Call To Reconciliation

We are so much like Peter. Jesus tells us what it will take to
follow him, and we want to argue. Jesus shows us the way to the
kingdom, and we seek a smoother path. Let us put down all that
keeps us from following Jesus, as we confess our sins to God.

Unison Prayer Of Confession

**We confess our struggle to be transformed into disciples,
God of Mystery. The desires of the world would shape us into
people you would not recognize. The demands of our society
pull us away from your heart. Our culture values the rich, the
powerful, and the successful, but you are on the side of the weak,
the poor, the outcast, and the oppressed.**

Forgive us, Merciful God, for looking for you in the wrong places. Reawaken us with your voice that calls us to service; revive our weary hearts with your vision of creation; refresh our fatigued spirits that we might boldly proclaim Jesus as our Lord and as our Savior, and go forth to serve your people in Christ's name.

Silence is kept

Assurance Of Pardon

One: It's too easy to think like the world, that money will give us happiness or that power will earn us grace. But Paul reminds us that if we think like Christ, and live like servants, we will find true freedom.

All: Not only our minds, but our hearts and spirits will be transformed into the likeness of Christ, enabling us to be faithful disciples. Thanks be to God. Amen.

Proper 17
Pentecost 15
Ordinary Time 22

Exodus 3:1-15
Romans 12:9-21
Matthew 16:21-28

Call To Worship

One: We are told that our love toward others
should be true and sincere,

**All: which is difficult toward those
who are mean, dishonest, and hateful.**

One: We are asked to love all people
as if they were our sisters and brothers,

**All: which suggests that all of us are one family,
there are to be no barriers between us.**

One: We are implored to be patient, to rejoice,
and to never stop praying,

**All: but we grow weary from our suffering,
our loneliness, and our grief.**

One: Why should we do all these things?

**All: Because we are God's people,
called to lives that are different,
and make the difference.**

Prayer Of The Day

God our Creator,
you are alive:
in the singing of geese flying south,
in the leaves gently stirring in the breeze,
in the stars that dance at night.

Christ, our Brother,
you are in our midst:
in the lap of a grandmother,
in the cries of a newborn,
in the stillness of dawn.

Spirit of God,
you make all ground holy:
the classes where we fidget,
the sidewalks where we meet our neighbors,
the grass in our backyards.

God in Community, Holy in One,
hear us now, as we pray as we have been taught,
    Our Father ...

Call To Reconciliation

Holy places are not far away; they are wherever we meet God. Burning bushes are not only found in stories, but in our homes, our workplaces, and our churches. We are so broken, we cannot see the sacred that surrounds us. Let us confess our sins to God, who desires nothing more than to forgive us.

Unison Prayer Of Confession

God of Moses and Miriam, your love for each of us can never be doubted, but our families and friends are often unsure of our affection for them. Your justice burns within us, God of Anna and Amos, but our frozen hearts cannot feel its touch. Your word would call us to lives of denial and service, God of Peter and Phoebe, but we cannot keep from looking out for ourselves before anyone else.

Forgive us, God of sinners and saints. We would hear your call to service; we would hear your challenge to deny ourselves; we would hear your invitation to faithfulness, and we will listen and follow our Lord and Savior, Jesus Christ.

Silence is kept

Assurance Of Pardon

One: This is the good news, my friends: God comes to give us new life, as forgiven and redeemed people.

All: **We sing our praises to the One who has made us whole. Thanks be to God. Amen.**

Proper 18
Pentecost 16
Ordinary Time 23

Exodus 12:1-14
Romans 13:8-14
Matthew 18:15-20

Call To Worship
One: To people held captive by others,
       to people overwhelmed by natural disasters,
       God calls us to be ready:
All: **ready to respond to those in need;**
       ready to respond to God's freedom.
One: To people whose friends persecute them,
       to people who are at odds with neighbors,
       Paul reminds us of our call to love:
All: **to love others as deeply as we love ourselves;**
       to love God with every fiber of our being.
One: For people who see the pain of the world,
       for people who know the brokenness of their lives,
       God provides a table:
All: **feeding us with grace and hope;**
       inviting us to eat as one family.

Prayer Of The Day
Liberating God,
you set us free from our loneliness
by the touch of another's hand;
you deliver us from our selfishness,
so we may serve others;
you break the chains of our pride,
that we might humbly walk with you.

Christ of Love,
when we would cling to our anger,
you send us forgiveness to hold our hand;
when we would feast on our bitterness,
you share the bread of heaven;
when we would drink at sin's fountain,
you pour out the cup of salvation.

Spirit of New Life,
you bring us together
that we might learn to live together,
to love together,
to serve together,
so that whose around us
would know you are in our midst.

God in Community, Holy in One,
we lift the prayer that Jesus has taught us, saying,
Our Father ...

Call To Reconciliation

In worship, in life, in every moment, Christ is among us: loving us, teaching us, leading us. But our focus on our needs, on our desires, keeps us from knowing his presence. Let us confess our sins against God and neighbor, as we pray,

Unison Prayer Of Confession

"Love one another." That is all you ask of us, Dear God. Yet we find this simple request so hard to carry out. Someone upsets us, and we curse them. Another buys something we want but cannot afford, and we are jealous. A friend gets recognition we wanted, and we talk about him or her behind his or her back.

Forgive us, Loving God, and free us from our slavery to sin. With Christ in our midst, we can become the people you dream about: loving, merciful, gentle, compassionate people of God.

Silence is kept

Assurance Of Pardon

One: Two, three, thirty, 300 — we have gathered as God's people; broken — we are made whole; alone — we are shaped into a family; forgiven — we are sent forth to serve.

All: **Fed, forgiven, restored, loved. The table is our constant reminder of God's presence in our lives, of God's grace that makes us new. Thanks be to God. Amen.**

Proper 19
Pentecost 17
Ordinary Time 24

Exodus 14:19-31
Romans 14:1-12
Matthew 18:21-35

Call To Worship

One: When we have been overwhelmed by the flood of fears,
        when our wheels got stuck in the mud,

All: **you were with us, O God,**
        helping us to find solid ground.

One: When we clung to our old securities,
        when we relied on the ways of the world,

All: **you went before us,**
        leading us into the kingdom of grace.

One: When we cling to everything that would hold us back,
        when we are hesitant to cut the ties to our past,

All: **you show us the future you have prepared for us;**
        you open our hearts to your love.

Prayer Of The Day

This is the place to which you have led us,
Cloud of Grace,
this sacred space
of memories and dreams,
of stories told to children,
of songs sung to you,
of gifts offered to others;
this home we call the church.

Christ of Tenderness,
when the foundation of our faith was being dug,
you used a shovel by our side;

169

when we stumble seeking to follow you,
you pick us up;
when the end of the journey seems uncertain,
you point us to the right path;
whatever we may face today or in the future,
you are with us.

Companion Spirit,
bless the people who are with us today:
those who inspire us, and those who irritate us;
those who make us laugh, and those who make us weep;
those whom we have known forever,
and those we have just met;
all who gather to be in this place with you.

God in Community, Holy in One,
hear us as we pray as Jesus has taught us, saying,
   Our Father ...

Call To Reconciliation

As we gather to praise God, we need to remember that we are
people who often resist God's way for us. But God is eager to
forgive us, and to strengthen us for discipleship. Let us confess our
sins to God, saying,

Unison Prayer Of Confession

**We admit how difficult it is for us to trust you, Living God.
The temptations, the desires, the calls of the world flood into
our lives, but we do not believe you can part them and lead us
into faithfulness. Our bitterness toward those who have hurt
us is like a feast we cannot leave, despite your invitation to the
table of grace and healing. Our grudges fit comfortably into
our hands, and if we let them go, we wonder if you will fill that
emptiness with hope.**

**Forgive us and have mercy on us. You are the God who
brought our ancestors into freedom — set us free from our
pain. You are the God who is with us in every moment — open
our eyes to your presence. You are the God of our future. In**

170

life, in death, you are with us, in Jesus Christ, our Lord and Savior.

Silence is kept

Assurance Of Pardon

One: God has claimed us and will not let us go. There is no one, there is no thing that can keep God from forgiving us, loving us, and healing us.

All: **Loved, we can love the unlovable;**
         graced, we can be a blessing to others;
         forgiven, we can forgive those who have hurt us.
         Thanks be to God. Amen.

Proper 20
Pentecost 18
Ordinary Time 25

Exodus 16:2-15
Philippians 1:21-30
Matthew 20:1-16

Call To Worship
One: Here, we gather in preparation
All: **calling on God's name,**
           singing praises to our Creator.
One: Here, we gather in anticipation
All: **believing that to live for Christ is gain;**
           to serve others in Christ is our calling.
One: Here, we gather in hope
All: **that God will take away our fears;**
           that the good news will transform our lives.

Prayer Of The Day
Like the dew on the grass,
Giver of Manna,
your grace comes to us
fresh each morning,
waiting to be gathered up,
savored with joy,
and shared with childish abandon.

Like the geese flying over our heads,
as we stand waiting for the bus,
you call to us,
Christ of Brokenness,
inviting us to set aside those desires
that fill us with a passion for ourselves,

172

and to take on that compassion
that reflects your heart for all who suffer.

Like the water that turns a desert into a spring,
Spirit of Generosity,
you flow into our lives,
taking the gift of God's holy emptiness
and filling it with prayer, with a song,
with a Word, with silence,
so that overflowing with the presence of Christ,
we can go forth to serve God's people.

God in Community, Holy in One,
hear us as we pray, saying,
Our Father ...

Call To Reconciliation

We try. God knows how hard we try. And God must wonder why we work so hard to earn love that is already ours, given joyfully, unconditionally, eternally. Set aside your weariness from working hard and come to receive God's healing mercy for your life. Please join me as we pray, saying,

Unison Prayer Of Confession

You frustrate us, Confusing God. We think we have you all neatly wrapped in a box, and you burst out with laughter on your lips and grace flowing from your heart. We grumble about how others seem to have more, forgetting how richly you have blessed us. We are hard pressed by the world to follow its seductive trail to empty hopes and false promises. We compete even with our best friends and closest neighbors, rather than offering encouragement and strength.

Forgive us, Providing God, for our failures to be your people. Help us to stop our grumbling, and to be bearers of grace to the broken; enable us to quit complaining and to share compassion with those who need healing and hope; teach us to sing, to sing of your glory, to sing of your mercy, to sing of your Son, Jesus Christ, our Lord and Savior, in whom we have life.

173

Silence is kept

Assurance Of Pardon

One: We expect to be condemned and receive compassion; we figure we will be punished, but are forgiven. God continually turns our world upside down, so we can live in joy and peace.

All: **By God's grace, we are new people;**
by God's Wisdom, we see others in a new light;
by God's Spirit, we serve in new ways.
Thanks be to God. Amen.

Proper 21
Pentecost 19
Ordinary Time 26

Exodus 17:1-7
Philippians 2:1-13
Matthew 21:23-32

Call To Worship

One: God became an infant
All: so we would become God's children.
One: God walked the earth, telling stories
All: so the words would guide our choices.
One: God became poor
All: so our riches would help others.
One: God became foolish
All: so we would be wise enough to follow.
One: God turned the world upside down
All: so we would find our way home.

Prayer Of The Day

You nourish us,
Rock-Splitter,
with grace flowing from hardened hearts,
and children splashing in fountains;
with stories we have heard from our grandparents
and parables we live out;
with intelligence that can cure a disease
and imagination that builds sand castles.

You challenge us,
Self-Emptier,
to let our minds be transformed by your love
and our love to be given away without logic;

to allow our stubborn will
to be transfigured into service;
to set down our selfishness
and stand with those who have nothing.

You fill us,
Sharing Spirit,
with compassion made real
when we stretch our hearts
in service to others;
with love offered to children
who need a lap to sit on;
with obedience that bends our knees
in worship to you.

God in Community, Holy in One,
to whom we pray as Jesus taught us, saying,
   Our Father ...

Call To Reconciliation

What do you think? There was a person who thought she had done nothing wrong, but whose heart is changed by God's grace and admits her mistakes. Another is always apologizing, but keeps on doing the same thing over and over. Which one is faithful to God's desires for us? Let us pause for a moment to think about this question and then pray together,

(pause)

Unison Prayer Of Confession
God of Glory,
our hearts are like rocks
that others strike with their needs;
   crack us open
   so our gifts may be poured out.

Our mistaken concept makes us think
we are better than those around us;
    humble us,
    so we might become
    servants to the world.
Our focus on ourselves makes us confident,
our needs, our interests, take priority over all else;
    fill our minds
    with Christ and his love,
    so we would think of others
    instead of ourselves.

Silence is kept

Assurance Of Pardon

One: Let this be firmly planted in your minds: God loves you; God forgives you; God strengthens you for service.

All: **May God's compassion make us more passionate to serve; may God's forgiveness make us eager to forgive; may God's love make us better lovers of the world. Thanks be to God. Amen.**

Proper 22
Pentecost 20
Ordinary Time 27

Exodus 20:1-4, 7-9, 12-20
Philippians 3:4b-14
Matthew 21:33-46

Call To Worship

One: All around us, the universe sings
of God's creative love.

**All: We gather as God's people,
seeking that love no one else can offer.**

One: Every day, the sun bears witness to God's hope;
every night, the stars whisper of God's peace.

**All: We gather as God's people,
needing peace in a warring world,
searching for hope in the midst of despair.**

One: The breath of the wind carries God's grace;
the mountains echo the glory of God.

**All: We gather as God's people,
from north and south,
from east and west,
to sit at the joyful feast.**

Prayer Of The Day

Composer of Heaven's Music,
with the eyes of compassion,
you see your children in bondage,
and redeem us;
with the voice of justice,
you create a people
urging us to live faithfully;

with a love that never ends,
you call us to be your body,
those who share your peace
with everyone we meet.

Jesus Christ,
Cornerstone of Creation,
you are the foundation of faith
that sustains us;
you are the voice of peace
that gives us hope;
you are the gift of life
that makes us God's own forever.

Spirit of Confidence,
you are the life-giving waters
that cleanse us of our fears;
you are the fire in our hearts
that burns for justice;
you are the wind of hope
that pushes us to serve others.

God in Community, Holy in One,
we gather in this place
to worship and adore you,
even as we pray as Jesus has taught us, saying,
Our Father ...

Call To Reconciliation

Like Paul, and so many before and after him, we think we are
made right with God by the number of rules we keep. Like Paul,
we need to realize we gain precisely what we need — forgiveness,
peace, hope — when we gain Jesus Christ as our Lord and Savior.
Let us confess our human ways that we might receive the loving
grace and mercy of the God who loves us.

Unison Prayer Of Confession

Hearer of our words and spirits, we know how we have not lived as your people these past days. We continue to carve idols of success, wealth, and power out of our stress. We find it easier to use your name in exasperation, rather than exaltation. We spread gossip about our closest friends, and it is hard to think of any thing we do not covet.

Forgive us, our Hearts' Best Thought. Hold our hidden faults to the light of Christ. Help us let go of what we value most, so we might grasp that which prizes us beyond anything in all creation — your love, your peace, your hope in us, through Jesus Christ, our Lord and Savior.

Silence is kept

Assurance Of Pardon

One: Not by anything we do, but by God's grace, we are forgiven. Our restoration to new life comes through faith in Christ, a faith beyond all value. This is, indeed, good news.

All: **We are prized, we are loved, we are forgiven. Thanks be to God. Amen.**

Proper 23
Pentecost 21
Ordinary Time 28

Exodus 32:1-14
Philippians 4:1-9
Matthew 22:1-14

Greeting

One: This is the day God has made.
All: Let us rejoice!
One: This is the day Christ rose from the dead.
All: Let us rejoice and be glad.
One: This day is the gift the Spirit offers to us.
All: Let us rejoice, and be glad in it.
One: And again, we say,
All: Rejoice!

Call To Worship

One: Who can tell of God's wonderful workings in our world?
All: Those who know they have been blessed
beyond their wildest imaginations.
One: Who can sing God's praises
to everyone they meet?
All: Those who have not forgotten
the joy of God's never-ending love in their lives.
One: Who can rejoice in God's presence,
this day, and in all the days to come?
All: Those who seek to grow in faith
and those who seek to share their gifts with God's
people.

Prayer Of The Day

Serene God,
take all the distractions of our lives
and set them to the side,
so we may focus on you;
silence the noise we have carried in with us,
so we may hear you;
unlock our closed hearts and minds,
so we may learn what it is you want to teach us.

Joyous Christ,
you tell us stories
not to make us feel guilty,
but to call us to servanthood;
you are as near
as the person sitting next to us,
as eager, as they,
to be our sister or brother.

Gentle Spirit,
fill us with your fire,
so we are aflame for justice;
fill us with your wisdom,
so we will know the deepest needs of others;
fill us with your compassion,
so our lives may be broken,
for our sisters and brothers.
Then we will rejoice in you always,

God in Community, Holy in One,
even as we pray as Jesus has taught us, saying,
   Our Father ...

Call To Reconciliation

Sin — according to the Bible — is the human condition. We sin, as did those who went before us and as will those who come after us. We do wrong, we hurt people, and we turn our backs on those who need us most. But God is able to turn our weeping into

182

rejoicing, and sinners into servants. Join me as we confess our sins to God, praying together, saying,

Unison Prayer Of Confession

Catering God, you would gather us at your banquet, but our hectic lives prevent us from attending. You encourage us to be gentle, but so often we are harsh toward those closest to us. What we have learned, we have forgotten; what we have received, we have misplaced; what we have heard and seen of you, we have ignored.

Forgive us, Table-Setting God. You pull out a chair for us, that we might feast on all that is true, all that is just, all that is honorable, all that is commendable — all your gifts served to us with joy and grace by Jesus Christ, our Lord and Savior.

Silence is kept

Assurance Of Pardon

One: In baptism, God lays hands of love and blessing on us — and never takes that tender touch from us. All around us are the wonders of creation, reminding us of God's grace and love.

All: **God invites us to the Wedding Feast with all its fullness, all its joy, and all its hope. This is good news: for each of us, for all of us. Thanks be to God. Amen.**

Charge

One: You are children of God.

All: **We will rejoice always;**
we will pray continually.

One: You are disciples of Christ.

All: **We are called to be caught**
in acts of stewardship.

One: You are heirs of the Spirit.

All: **We will keep on doing the things**
we have learned and received
and heard and seen.

Proper 24
Pentecost 22
Ordinary Time 29

Exodus 33:12-23
1 Thessalonians 1:1-10
Matthew 22:15-22

Call To Worship

One: We gather in God's holy presence,
      coming to the One who knows us by name.

**All: God's glory surprises us each morning;
       God's goodness cradles us at night when we sleep.**

One: We praise the One whose justice is for all;
      whose word transforms every life.

**All: God's presence never leaves us;
       God's mercy mends the cracks in our broken lives.**

One: We give thanks to God for the hope of each day;
      we remember God's splendor lighting our way.

**All: God's compassion walks with us every moment;
       God's grace is the air we breathe.**

Prayer Of The Day

Honest God,
we want to see your glory,
so you reveal your goodness to us;
we want a taste of your power,
so you offer us your broken child;
we want to know your truth,
so you come to us in love.

Light of Truth,
your faithfulness to God's call
reveals the seductiveness
of the idols we worship;

your plain talk whispers to us
over the songs of our society;
your words carve honesty
on our misshapen hearts.

Truth-Speaker,
you alone can reveal the lies
that the evil one would tell us;
you caress us with genuine compassion,
so we can become love's servants;
you embrace us with candor,
so we can speak the words of hope
the world strains to hear.

Holy and True God,
Perfect in Community,
hear us as we pray as Jesus taught us, saying,
    Our Father ...

Call To Reconciliation

When we hear the truth, it seems so simple that it amazes us.
Yet, scripture is clear, that God desires to forgive us, to heal us, and
to give us new life. Keep this truth in mind, as we confess together
our sins, saying,

Unison Prayer Of Confession

**Mighty King, Lover of Justice, we confess we are cowards
when it comes to accepting new truths; lazily, we content ourselves with half-truths; arrogantly, we think we know all truth;
and so we slide into lives where lies are easily spoken, honesty
is held up to scorn, and sincerity is mocked.**

**Forgive us, Good Lord, forgive us. Let us expose the dark
sides of our souls to the light of your grace; let us discover the
sin that has been stowed away in our hearts and cast it into
your sea of forgetfulness; let us see your goodness — our Lord
and Savior, Jesus Christ, going before us, so we can follow him
into your kingdom.**

Silence is kept

Assurance Of Pardon

One: I share the good news with you — God desires to be gracious to us, to forgive us, to choose us to be the people who will share this truth with all people.

All: **We hear, we believe, we will live out this good news in our lives. Thanks be to God. Amen.**

Proper 25
Pentecost 23
Ordinary Time 30

Deuteronomy 34:1-12
1 Thessalonians 2:1-8
Matthew 22:34-46

Call To Worship

One: God, enlarge our hearts,
**All: so we can become compassionate enough
to serve our neighbors.**
One: God, broaden our minds,
**All: so we may discern you
in everyone we meet.**
One: God, deepen our souls,
**All: so we may continually overflow
with your grace.**
One: God, fill us with your love,
**All: so we may be grateful enough
to share it each and every day.**

Prayer Of The Day

Creation's Witness,
when our dreams fade,
your hope paints a new future for us;
when our eyes grow dim to your love,
your gentleness watches over us
like a nanny caring for her own children;
when our hearts turn to ice,
your grace warms us
like a shawl on a chilly day.

Word of Love,
you answer every question,

even the ones buried in our souls;
you speak good news to us,
trusting we will tell it
to everyone we know,
singing its joy in all moments.

Wisdom from generation to generation,
from the time
you first wound creation's clock,
to its last tick,
you are with us,
caring deeply for us,
dwelling in our hearts,
lighting us with the fire of hope.

God in Community, Holy in One,
hear us as we pray as we have been taught, saying,
   Our Father ...

Call To Reconciliation

God never tires of giving us chances to offer others love and hope, but we throw away such moments when we deny mercy, withhold love, or cling to our wealth. God never grows weary of loving us enough to forgive us, so join me as we pray together, saying,

Unison Prayer Of Confession

Your love, Steadfast God, is like a never-ending stream filled with family, with friends, and with you. We water down our love for others with greed, with envy, and with self-interest. Our love for you is often based on what we think you will give us.

Have mercy on us, Watchful God, and forgive us. Help us learn to love humbly, gracefully, generously, and compassionately. Add our drops of love to your river that flows to all people through the heart of Jesus Christ, our Lord and Savior.

Silence is kept

Assurance Of Pardon

One: We no longer have to wait. God fills us with compassion and steadfast love, this morning, and every day to come.

All: **God's joy, God's hope, God's grace rests upon us and prepares us to go forth sharing these gifts — with our family, our friends, our neighbors, with all of God's people. Thanks be to God. Amen.**

Charge

One: And now, go forth — to love God with all your heart, your mind, your soul,

All: **with passion, with prayer, and with intelligence.**

One: Go forth to love your neighbor,

All: **with forgiveness, with service, with love,**

One: and to love yourself

All: **with hope, with joy, and with peace.**

Reformation Sunday

Jeremiah 31:31-34
Romans 3:19-28
John 8:31-36

Call To Worship
One: Be still!
All: We come to quiet ourselves in this haven of holiness.
One: Be still and know ...
All: We come to discern the word that can set us free.
One: Be still and know that God is
All: our Hope, our Help, our Refuge, and our Redeemer.

Prayer Of The Day
You break the cycle of wars,
so we may be enriched by your peace;
you shatter the grip of violence,
so we may be freed from our fears;
you plant your words of hope deep within us,
carving on our hearts:
"You Are Mine."
You give us the word we need,
so we might live in your grace,
God of Creation.

You freely become one of us,
so we could be liberated from our addiction to sin;
you take us by the hand
to lead us out of our doubts;
you give us the words we need,
so we can continue to share your good news of life,
Friend of the Needy.

You pull us to safety
when sin's waters swirl around our feet;

you surround us with serenity
when doubts rattle our souls;
you give us words we need,
whenever we wander
onto the paths of trouble,
Spirit of Holiness.

God of Community, Holy in One,
you give us the words we need
to pray as Jesus has taught us, saying,
Our Father ...

Call To Reconciliation

We can no longer flatter ourselves about how good we are. We do not need to make grandstand plays to get God's attention. We only need to confess our lives, as God makes good on the promises of grace and mercy.

Unison Prayer Of Confession

Heart of the Covenant: We have known your hopes for us, and disappointed every one of them; we have heard your words of faithfulness, and broken every one of them; we have seen your dreams for us, and turned them all into nightmares.

Forgive us, Hope's Heart. Silence every blustering word, so we may hear your mercy; still every feeble attempt to justify ourselves, so we may be made right with you; melt every frozen heart, so we might be drenched in your river of joy. May Jesus Christ continue to live in us, so we might be free to live forever with you.

Silence is kept

Assurance Of Pardon

One: Be still and know the good news: God has not forsaken nor
      forgotten us, but redeems us.
All: **Why should we be afraid! God is in our midst — forgiving, restoring, sending. Thanks be to God! Amen.**

191

All Saints

Revelation 7:9-17
1 John 3:1-3
Matthew 5:1-12

Call To Worship

One: At all times we are called
to bless God's name.

**All: Our lips drench with praises,
our hearts exult in God.**

One: The proud will bend knees in worship,
the humble will lift glad songs.

**All: We are set free from our fears,
we have searched for God and been found.**

One: Our faces glow with thanksgiving,
our spirits overflow with grace.

**All: God has wiped away our tears,
God has fed us from the storehouses of hope.**

Prayer Of The Day

They are gathered around you,
God of Forever and Ever.
Some are well known,
like Martin Luther,
Mother Teresa,
C. S. Lewis,
Helen Keller,
and so many more.
Some have been forgotten,
like Agnes and Cadoc,
Tuda, Mary of Egypt,
and Ebba,
while others have days named after them.

But many are ordinary folk,
such as the teacher from second grade
who guided our fingers under the words;
the nurse in the hospital
who held our hand while blood was taken;
the coach who trusted us with the ball,
not the end of the bench.

There is an old man who left retirement behind him,
and an barren woman who laughed at your promise;
there are popes, princes, and power-brokers,
who are taught heaven's hymns
by the paupers and pretenders;
there are those who moved mountains
and those who murmured in the wilderness;
there are those who founded the church,
and those who floundered on the waves of Galilee.

All saints,
just like us,
singing your praise forever and ever,
and we join in their anthem
even as we pray as Jesus has taught us, saying,
Our Father ...

Call To Reconciliation
When God sets the table of the Lamb, all will be welcome —
the young and the old; those who were faithful, and those who
failed; those who followed Jesus, and those who lost their way. Let
us confess to God our unsaintly ways, knowing how quick God is
to forgive.

Unison Prayer Of Confession
We did not listen, when the Teacher spoke, God of Sinners.
Rich in pride and arrogance,
our spirits have no need for a kingdom;
taught to not let anyone see us cry,

193

we refuse your comforting arms;
seeing the rich and successful have their way,
we yearn to inherit their hardened hearts;
noticing the hungry standing by the side of the road,
we make sure we get more than our share of the world's
resources;
taking note of how he merciful are pushed aside,
we develop callouses on our souls.

Forgive us, Saint Maker, that we follow the wrong examples and listen to false teachings. It is the peacemakers who live into your hope; it is those whose hearts are shaped by yours, who are able to see you in the poor and broken; it is those who give themselves to serve others who are your saints, following the example of Jesus Christ, our Lord, our Savior, our Shepherd, guiding us to the wellsprings of life.

Silence is kept

Assurance Of Pardon

One: When we seek God, we are found;
       when we cry out, we are heard;
       when we confess, we are forgiven and made new.
All: **We can taste the yeasty flavor of grace, we can drink the deep wine of hope, we can find our home in God's heart receiving mercy and new life. Thanks be to God. Amen.**

Proper 26
Pentecost 24
Ordinary Time 31

Joshua 3:7-17
1 Thessalonians 2:9-13
Matthew 23:1-12

Call To Worship

One: Some have come a great distance,
          others have just crossed the street.
All: We come with joy in our hearts
          for God's love is always, always with us.
One: Some have wandered far from home,
          others have stuck to the straight way.
All: We come because God has gathered us here,
          so we might find hope and grace.
One: Some are hungry for that word that can transform,
          others thirst for that Companion who will never desert them.
All: We come, knowing our search is ended,
          finally finding ourselves at home.

Prayer Of The Day

Creation's Guide,
at the birth of time,
you gave us life,
and continue to pour out this gift upon us.
Parched by the bitterness of our lives,
you offer us a drink
from the wellsprings of your heart;
tempted to listen to society's seductive whispers,
you plead with us
to cross the river
to that land called promise.

World's Wanderer,
when we stumble
through this weary wilderness,
you take us by the hand,
so we might get back
on the path of faithfulness;
when we are about to grasp
the power of pride,
you call us to serve others.

Life's Companion,
when we stand at the river's edge,
hesitant to dip our toes in to test the waters,
you come up behind us and push us in,
so we might be immersed
in your joy.

God in Community, Holy in One,
we rejoice in your tender presence,
even as we pray as Jesus has taught us, saying,
    Our Father ...

Call To Reconciliation
    When Jesus criticizes how the religious people of his time acted,
we discover he is talking about us. Yet, Jesus is also the One who
comes, that we might discover the forgiveness and hope offered to
us by our God. Let us confess our sins, as we pray together, saying,

Unison Prayer Of Confession
    **In a society that worships authority, Guiding God, we find
it awkward to be servants. In a world that exalts achievements
and pride, it is hard to be humble. In a time in which the indi-
vidual reigns supreme, how difficult it is to lead lives of sacrifice on behalf of others!**
    **Forgive us, Patient God, deliver us from our worst selves,
so we might be better disciples; turn our empty despair into
springs of hope for others; lead us down the path to your**

kingdom, every step shaped by the One we follow, Jesus Christ, our Teacher, our Lord, our Savior.

Silence is kept

Assurance Of Pardon

One: This is the good news: God loves us, God forgives us, God calls us to lives poured out for others.

All: **In Jesus Christ, we are forgiven so we might become servants to those in need. Thanks be to God. Amen.**

Proper 27
Pentecost 25
Ordinary Time 32

Joshua 24:1-3a, 14-25
1 Thessalonians 4:13-18
Matthew 25:1-13

Call To Worship

One: If we will but listen,

All: God will speak to us in parables;
God will tell us stories lived out by our grandparents.

One: If we will but remember,

All: we will discover all we have heard and known;
all the wonders God has in store for us.

One: If we will but share,

All: we can tell our children and grandchildren —
even those not yet born —
the glorious stories of our God.

Prayer Of The Day

We stand at the crossing,
Holy God,
arms, hearts, souls,
full of the burdens
the gods of this world
have placed on us.
You remove them,
throw them to one side,
taking us by the hand
to lead us into your kingdom.

As we turn to you in our despair,
Holy Friend,
you come and fill our emptiness

with the holy oil of your compassion,
so we might always
be ready to serve
those who come to us.

Holy Wisdom,
you would not leave us
uninformed of God's love for us,
so you whisper in our ears
of the wonders beyond our dreaming;
you remove the blindfold from our eyes
to behold the grace flowing around us;
you open our hearts
to the family God has given us.

God in Community, Holy in One,
hear us as we pray as Jesus has taught us, saying,
Our Father ...

Call To Reconciliation

How quickly we forget — our faith, our calling, our hope. All because we try to do everything our way, rather than God's. But God is quicker to forgive, and to restore us to new life. Let us confess to our God, as we pray, saying,

Unison Prayer Of Confession

It is never easy to admit how foolish we are, Approaching God. You have chosen us for yourself, and we continue to shelter false gods in our hearts. You promise to be with us in every moment, but we can find little time for you. You send your word to us, but we are too busy listening to the noise of our culture to pay attention.

Have mercy, Eternal One, and forgive us. Speak to us, so we might listen, and in hearing, be transformed into your people. Fill us with holiness, so we might give ourselves wholly to others. Enable us to serve you faithfully and completely, even as did our Lord and Savior, Jesus Christ.

Silence is kept

Assurance Of Pardon

One: This is our assurance: God forgives us.
          This is our hope: God's love is everlasting.
          This is our truth: God is with us always.

All: **We will speak the truth;**
          we will live the hope;
          we will share God's forgiveness.
          Thanks be to God. Amen.

Proper 28
Pentecost 26
Ordinary Time 33

Judges 4:1-7
1 Thessalonians 5:1-11
Matthew 25:14-30

Call To Worship
One: Before there was any time,
All: there was God.
One: When we wandered through the wilderness,
All: God built the way for us.
One: When we lived in exile,
All: our homes were built by God.
One: When we are overwhelmed by stress and change,
All: God unknots the tightness in our shoulders.
One: When we seek to serve faithfully,
All: God provides the opportunities.
One: When tomorrow comes,
All: we find God awake and waiting for us.
One: When time ends,
All: there will still be God.

Prayer Of The Day
Conqueror of Chaos,
you reached down
gathering up the dust,
filling it with your breath,
and giving us life.
We gather in worship
so we might continue
to be shaped by your love.

You walked the paths
of dusty earth,
Christ our Servant,
lifting us up when we had fallen,
feeding us when we were famished,
healing us when we were broken, and
saving us when we were sinners.

Spirit of Hope,
you laugh,
and leaves dance down the streets;
you whisper,
and children sleep in peace;
you clap your hands,
and our souls leap with joy.

God in Community, Holy in One,
we lift our prayers to you,
using the words taught to us by the Christ, saying,
Our Father ...

Call To Reconciliation

God created us for goodness, and too often we make the wrong choices. God, who walked this earth, knows our temptations. God, whose hope is for wholeness, waits to forgive us. Let us come to our God, as we confess our sins together, saying,

Unison Prayer Of Confession

God of Promises, you offer us guidance, and we rush to grasp the hand of our world. You would nurture us with love and grace, and we feast on the empty calories of success and seduction. You call us to be your faithful people, and we are eager to follow the politicians, the promoters, and the petty.

Forgive us, Covenant God. You have not forgotten your promises, nor will you break them. Rather, you come to us so we might know your love; you walk with us, so we might find our way; you redeem us so we might trust that promises have

been fulfilled once and for all in Jesus Christ, our Lord and Savior.

Silence is kept

Assurance Of Pardon

One: In every time and in every place, God shows compassion and mercy. Thus, we know God has heard our prayers and has filled us with forgiveness and hope.

All: **In this time, in this place, we are filled with grace and sustained by love. Thanks be to God, we are forgiven. Amen.**

Christ The King
Proper 29

Ezekiel 34:11-16, 20-24
Ephesians 1:15-23
Matthew 25:31-46

Call To Worship
One: We come — scatterbrained, fractured by work,
       stressed and strained beyond limit.
All: **God gathers us up and brings up to this place,**
       the kingdom of healing and peace.
One: We come — scoffers of wisdom, skeptics of sainthood,
       questioners of confessions and creeds.
All: **God collects us in the power of the Word,**
       reminding us that we are never lost.
One: We come — mockers of motives, disbelievers in justice,
       rogues about righteousness.
All: **God scoops us up from every street corner**
       and brings us home with our sisters and brothers.

Prayer Of The Day
You search for us
when we are lost,
and bring us home,
Master of the Universe.
Our scattered thoughts
are knitted together
by your grace
so we might know,
beyond any doubt,
that you are God.

Word-Bearer of Hope,
we wander the deserts of desire,
and question why we are parched;
we feast on the scraps
of the table set by trouble,
and cannot imagine being filled;
we cling to every blessing
you have given to us,
and call ourselves impoverished.

Spirit of Wisdom,
reveal to us our brokenness,
so we might become whole;
enlighten our hearts,
so we can be more loving;
show us the path
from which we have strayed,
so we can find our way home.

God in Community, Holy in One,
we lift the prayer Jesus has taught us, saying,
    Our Father ...

Call To Reconciliation

None of us think we are lost — but the shadows of the world seduce us. None of us have strayed, though we often refuse to ask for directions. When we confess our real situation and reveal who we are, we discover the One who has been searching for us. Please join me, as we pray together, saying,

Unison Prayer Of Confession

We like to pat ourselves on the back for all the good things we do, Pursuing God. We give a canned good to the food pantry; we drop an old coat in the collection barrel; we send a note to someone in the hospital. But when we look over our shoulders, we see you emptying out your refrigerator, pushing a cart filled with new clothes for the homeless, sitting by the bedside of a cancer patient in the loneliest hours of the morning.

205

You go to the ends of the earth to forgive us, Merciful God, and to the very depths of death itself to give us new life. May we have the faith to live as your people, and the wisdom to share from the riches you have given us, in Jesus Christ, our Lord and Savior.

Silence is kept

Assurance Of Pardon

One: God seeks the lost —
All: that's us;
One: God adopts the strays of the world —
All: that's us;
One: God strengthens the weak —
All: that's us;
One: God forgives all who fail —
All: that's us! Thanks be to God. Amen.

Thanksgiving Day

Deuteronomy 8:7-18
2 Corinthians 9:6-15
Luke 17:11-19

Call To Worship
One: Our help is in the name of the Lord
          who made the heavens and earth.
All: **We glorify our God**
          with songs of thanksgiving and joy.
One: We will not forget
          all that God has done,
All: **feeding our grandparents with manna,**
          quenching our thirst with streams of living water.
One: We will not forget to speak the simple words,
          "Thank you!" to our God.
All: **As we sing and shout together**
          of God's amazing love.

Prayer Of The Day
Hot showers in the morning
and cool breezes in the evening;
work that provides for our families,
and abundance that makes us generous;
silly jokes told by third graders,
and the silent tears of a grandmother
lost in her childhood forever.
What blessings are ours,
Creation's Joy!

Teachers who patiently help us with our math,
and mentors who keep us on the right paths;
friends who shovel snow off sidewalks before we waken,
and employers whose hearts are greater than their profits;

piano teachers who smile at our repeated mistakes,
coaches who teach us (one more time)
how to curl the ball into the goal.
What blessings are ours,
Servant of Joy!

Dogs who bounce us awake early in the day
and cats who lullaby us to sleep at night;
grandfathers who teach us how to whittle
and sisters who give up a date to babysit;
little boys who always forget to wipe their mouths
and folks who always remember to say, "Thank you."
What blessings are ours,
Joyous Spirit!

God in Community, Holy in One,
thanksgiving is in every word we speak,
even as we pray as Jesus taught us, saying,
    Our Father ...

Call To Reconciliation

    How easily we think it is our power, our skills, our selves that
have given us what we have. In our feasts of self-exaltation, we no
longer remember the One who is giver of all we need. Let us confess our sins, as we pray, saying,

Unison Prayer Of Confession

    **Because we live in this modern, tech-savvy, instant-mes-
saging world, we forget how much we need you, Blessing God.
We exalt ourselves on our skills in surfing the internet, yet forget the One who hears our prayers before we open our hearts.
Because grocery stores have more than we could ever hope to
eat, we forget your waters that nurtured the food in our bas-
kets. Because our closets spill over with clothes we never wear,
we cannot see the meadows garbed in your radiant joy.**

    **Forgive us, Gracious Creator. Enriching us with blessings,
make us generous spenders of your grace on others. With our
hands full of treasures beyond imagining, may we think of new**

208

ways to share them. Feasting on your constant love, may we learn to love others more than ourselves, even as our Lord and Savior, Jesus Christ, loved us more than he loved his own life.

Silence is kept

Assurance Of Pardon

One: This is the good news for you: God provides every blessing; God forgives every sin; God delivers every one of us.

All: **So simple, yet so hard to say, "Thank you"**
for grace,
for hope,
for new life,
for new ways to serve.
Thank you, Holy God! We are forgiven. Amen.

Holy Humor Sunday

*(**Note:** An ancient tradition is to celebrate the resurrection of Jesus Christ with parties, laughter, joy, and celebrations. In some traditions, the entire first week of Eastertide was filled with such events. Others celebrated the second Sunday of Easter as "Bright" Sunday, the day to tell jokes, and to laugh about the great joke God pulled on the evil one by raising Jesus from the dead. What follows is a liturgy for what many today call Holy Humor Sunday.)*

Call To Worship

One: This is the time to rejoice!

All: **What better time than now!**

One: This is the day to laugh:
        What did the cabbage pastor say to the people?

Pastor: Lettuce pray!

One: How many choir directors does it take to change a light bulb?

Choir: No one knows, because no one ever watches the director!

One: How many [insert denomination here] does it take to change a light bulb?

All: **Change? [insert denomination here] don't believe in change!**

One: What's the greatest joke ever?

All: **The one God played Easter morning on death!**

Prayer Of The Day

You smiled and the sun burst
through the shadows of chaos;
you chuckled,
and the platypus splashed
in creation's fountain;
you laughed,
and all that is good and beautiful

was given shape by you,
Imaginative God.

Snickering at the feeble attempts
of the evil one,
you showed us
how to resist temptation;
giggling at sin's desperate desire
to hold onto us,
you released us by your love;
howling with laughter
at death's foolish belief
that the tomb could hold you,
you burst forth into the kingdom
as the stars pealed with joy,
Laughing Jesus.

As you fill us with new life,
may we delight in sharing it with others;
as you tell us the good news
which can never be taken from us,
may we rejoice in offering it
to the broken, the sad, the lonely;
as you tickle us with grace,
may we give it away with laughter on our lips
and joy in our hearts,
Spirit of Easter.

God in Community, Holy in One,
our hearts overflow with wonder
as we lift the prayer Jesus has taught us,
   Our Father ...

Call To Reconciliation

None of us likes to look foolish, but which is sillier? Chasing after the world and all its gaudy trinkets that flatter our souls, or being a "fool for Christ"; imitating him in service to others, offering ourselves in love and joy to the world? Let us admit to God the foolish choices we make each and every day, as we pray, saying,

212

Unison Prayer Of Confession

You know better than we do, Amused God, what important people we believe we are. Believing we have to be serious all the time, we miss out on the joy of your creation. Choosing to feast on the pain of the world, we skip the picnic offered in paradise. Clinging to the despair that is our best friend, we ignore Jesus, who can bring us home to your heart.

Forgive us, Heart of Joy, and make us open to the startling, and upside-down, ways in which you work. Fill us with Easter's laughter; fill us with your healing joy; fill us with the love poured into us through Jesus Christ, our Lord and Savior.

Silence is kept

Assurance Of Pardon

One: The gospels tell us over and over again of the joy that comes to us through Christ. When Jesus was around, lives were changed, the sick were healed, and the sorrowful began to laugh with joy. The good news is that this joy is now given to us.

All: **Through the Holy Spirit, we are gifted with joy. We are sent forth to bring good news to the oppressed, to bring healing to the broken, and to anoint everyone with the oil of gladness. Thanks be to God.**

213

US/Canadian Lectionary Comparison

The following index shows the correlation between the Sundays and special days of the church year as they are titled or labeled in the Revised Common Lectionary published by the Consultation On Common Texts and used in the United States (the reference used for this book) and the Sundays and special days of the church year as they are titled or labeled in the Revised Common Lectionary used in Canada.

Revised Common Lectionary	Canadian Revised Common Lectionary
Advent 1	Advent 1
Advent 2	Advent 2
Advent 3	Advent 3
Advent 4	Advent 4
Christmas Eve	Christmas Eve
The Nativity Of Our Lord/ Christmas Day	The Nativity Of Our Lord
Christmas 1	Christmas 1
January 1/New Year's Day	January 1/The Name Of Jesus
Christmas 2	Christmas 2
The Epiphany Of Our Lord	The Epiphany Of Our Lord
The Baptism Of Our Lord/ Epiphany 1	The Baptism Of Our Lord/ Proper 1
Epiphany 2/Ordinary Time 2	Epiphany 2/Proper 2
Epiphany 3/Ordinary Time 3	Epiphany 3/Proper 3
Epiphany 4/Ordinary Time 4	Epiphany 4/Proper 4
Epiphany 5/Ordinary Time 5	Epiphany 5/Proper 5
Epiphany 6/Ordinary Time 6	Epiphany 6/Proper 6
Epiphany 7/Ordinary Time 7	Epiphany 7/Proper 7
Epiphany 8/Ordinary Time 8	Epiphany 8/Proper 8
The Transfiguration Of Our Lord/ Last Sunday After Epiphany	The Transfiguration Of Our Lord/ Last Sunday After Epiphany
Ash Wednesday	Ash Wednesday
Lent 1	Lent 1
Lent 2	Lent 2
Lent 3	Lent 3
Lent 4	Lent 4
Lent 5	Lent 5
Passion/Palm Sunday	Passion/Palm Sunday
Maundy Thursday	Holy/Maundy Thursday
Good Friday	Good Friday

Easter Day	The Resurrection Of Our Lord
Easter 2	Easter 2
Easter 3	Easter 3
Easter 4	Easter 4
Easter 5	Easter 5
Easter 6	Easter 6
The Ascension Of Our Lord	The Ascension Of Our Lord
Easter 7	Easter 7
The Day Of Pentecost	The Day Of Pentecost
The Holy Trinity	The Holy Trinity
Proper 4/Pentecost 2/O T 9*	Proper 9
Proper 5/Pent 3/O T 10	Proper 10
Proper 6/Pent 4/O T 11	Proper 11
Proper 7/Pent 5/O T 12	Proper 12
Proper 8/Pent 6/O T 13	Proper 13
Proper 9/Pent 7/O T 14	Proper 14
Proper 10/Pent 8/O T 15	Proper 15
Proper 11/Pent 9/O T 16	Proper 16
Proper 12/Pent 10/O T 17	Proper 17
Proper 13/Pent 11/O T 18	Proper 18
Proper 14/Pent 12/O T 19	Proper 19
Proper 15/Pent 13/O T 20	Proper 20
Proper 16/Pent 14/O T 21	Proper 21
Proper 17/Pent 15/O T 22	Proper 22
Proper 18/Pent 16/O T 23	Proper 23
Proper 19/Pent 17/O T 24	Proper 24
Proper 20/Pent 18/O T 25	Proper 25
Proper 21/Pent 19/O T 26	Proper 26
Proper 22/Pent 20/O T 27	Proper 27
Proper 23/Pent 21/O T 28	Proper 28
Proper 24/Pent 22/O T 29	Proper 29
Proper 25/Pent 23/O T 30	Proper 30
Proper 26/Pent 24/O T 31	Proper 31
Proper 27/Pent 25/O T 32	Proper 32
Proper 28/Pent 26/O T 33	Proper 33
Christ The King (Proper 29/O T 34)	Proper 34/Christ The King/ Reign Of Christ
Reformation Day (October 31)	Reformation Day (October 31)
All Saints (November 1 or 1st Sunday in November)	All Saints' Day (November 1)
Thanksgiving Day (4th Thursday of November)	Thanksgiving Day (2nd Monday of October)

*O T = Ordinary Time

WARNING
Removing or tampering with the card on the back side of this page renders this book non-returnable.

Title: Lectionary Worship Aids, Series VIII, Cycle A

ISBN: 0-7880-2456-6

INSTRUCTIONS TO ACCESS PASSWORD FOR ELECTRONIC COPY OF THIS TITLE:

The password appears on the reverse side of this page. Carefully cut the card from the page to retireve the password.

Once you have the password, go to

http:/www.csspub.com/passwords/

and locate this title on that web page. By clicking on the title, you will be guided to a page to enter your password, name, and email address. From there you will be sent to a page to download your electronic version of this book.

For further information, or if you don't have access to the internet, please contact CSS Publishing Company at 1-800-241-4056 in the United States (or 419-227-1818 from outside the United States) between 8 a.m. and 5 p.m., Eastern Standard Time, Monday through Friday.